The Coaching Relationship

The Coaching Relationship discusses how we can integrate process perspectives, such as the quality of the coach–coachee relationship, and professional perspectives, including the influences of training and supervision, for more effective outcomes.

Stephen Palmer and Almuth McDowall bring together experts from the field of coaching to discuss different aspects of the coach–coachee relationship, topics covered including:

- the interpersonal perspective
- the role of assessment
- ethical issues
- cultural influences
- issues of power.

The book also includes a chapter on the interpersonal relationship in the training and supervision of coachès to provide a complete overview of how the coaching relationship can contribute to successful coaching

Illustrated throughout with case studies and client dialogue, *The Coaching Relationship* is essential reading for practising coaches and coaching psychologists wishing to learn more about the interpersonal aspects of coaching.

Stephen Palmer is Honorary Professor of Psychology at City University and Director of the Coaching Psychology Unit. He is Founder Director of the Centre for Coaching, London.

Almuth McDowall is Lecturer in Psychology at Surrey University and an independent practitioner for both the private and the public sector.

Essential Coaching Skills and Knowledge
Series Editors: Gladeana McMahon, Stephen Palmer & Averil Leimon

The **Essential Coaching Skills and Knowledge** series provides an accessible and lively introduction to key areas in the developing field of coaching. Each title in the series is written by leading coaches with extensive experience and has a strong practical emphasis, including illustrative vignettes, summary boxes, exercises and activities. Assuming no prior knowledge, these books will appeal to professionals in business, management, human resources, psychology, counselling and psychotherapy, as well as students and tutors of coaching and coaching psychology.

www.routledgementalhealth.com/essential-coaching-skills

Titles in the series:

The Coaching Relationship

Putting People First

*Edited by Stephen Palmer &
Almuth McDowall*

Routledge
Taylor & Francis Group

LONDON AND NEW YORK

First published 2010
by Routledge
27 Church Lane, Hove, East Sussex BN3 2FA

Simultaneously published in the USA and Canada
by Routledge
270 Madison Avenue, New York, NY 10016

Routledge is an imprint of the Taylor & Francis Group, an Informa business

Typeset in New Century Schoolbook by
RefineCatch Limited, Bungay, Suffolk
Printed and bound in Great Britain by
TJ International Ltd, Padstow, Cornwall
Paperback cover design by Lisa Dynan

British Library Cataloguing in Publication Data
A catalogue record for this book is available from the British Library

Library of Congress Cataloging-in-Publication Data

The coaching relationship : putting people first / edited by Stephen Palmer & Almuth McDowall.
  p. cm.
  Includes bibliographical references and index.
  ISBN 978–0–415–45873–3 (hbk) – ISBN 978–0–415–45874–0 (pbk)
1. Employees—Coaching of.   I. Palmer, Stephen, 1955–   II. McDowall, Almuth, 1966–
  HF5549.5.C53C636 2010
  658.3′124–dc22

                            2009030775

                        ISBN: 978–0–415–45873–3 (hbk)
                        ISBN: 978–0–415–45874–0 (pbk)

To

Frank and Sylvie Gillham (SP)

and

Rhiannon Rosalie McDowall (AM)

Contents

Editors and contributors

Editors

Stephen Palmer is a Psychologist, an APECS Accredited Executive Coach and Supervisor, and an Accredited Therapist. He is Founder Director of the Coaching Psychology Unit at City University, and Director of the Centre for Coaching, London. He is Honorary President of the Society for Coaching Psychology and Honorary Vice President of the International Stress Management Association (UK). He has written or edited 35 books including the *Handbook of Coaching Psychology: A Guide for Practitioners* (with Whybrow, 2007). In 2008, the British Psychological Society's Special Group in Coaching Psychology gave him the 'Lifetime Achievement Award in Recognition of Distinguished Contribution to Coaching Psychology', awarded at the 1st European Coaching Psychology Conference.

Almuth McDowall is an Occupational Psychologist who combines a full-time academic post at Surrey University with freelance work as an independent practitioner for both the private and the public sector. Her main research and practice interests are work/life balance, feedback, coaching and cross-cultural assessments. Almuth has published in the academic and in the practitioner press, and is a regular speaker at national and international conferences.

Contributors

Tatiana Bachkirova is an Occupational Psychologist who works as a coaching supervisor and academic at Oxford Brookes University. She is an active researcher and Co-Editor-in-Chief of *Coaching: An International Journal of Theory, Research and Practice.*

Elaine Cox is Head of the Coaching and Mentoring Research Group at Oxford Brookes University. She has been coaching and mentoring for over 14 years, working mainly in the voluntary and public sector and is the Editor of the open access *International Journal of Evidence-Based Coaching and Mentoring.* Elaine is also the author of a number of book chapters and journal articles and is currently co-editing *The Sage Handbook of Coaching.*

Lina Daouk-Öyry is Assistant Professor in Management, Marketing and Entrepreneurship track at Suliman S. Olayan School of Business at the American University of Beirut. Her areas of interest are in organisational behaviour and in occupational and educational assessment in cross-cultural contexts.

Peter Hawkins, Joint Founder (1986) and Chair of Bath Consultancy Group, is a leading consultant, writer and researcher in organisational strategy, culture, leadership and executive coaching and specialises in managing complex change and development. He has worked with many leading companies throughout the world, co-designing and facilitating major change and organisational transformation projects and developing senior executives and board members. He has been a keynote speaker at a number of international conferences on the learning organisation, leadership and executive coaching and teaches and leads master-classes at a number of business schools. He is a Visiting Professor at the University of Bath, and has also taught at a wide variety of universities both in the UK and in South Africa. Currently, Peter is Honorary President of the Association of Professional Executive Coaches and Supervisors and a member of the Advisory Board of the University of Bath's School of

Management. He was voted runner-up as the most influential person in coaching in 2007.

Ho Law is a Registered Psychologist in the UK, the 2010 Chair of BPS SGCP, President, Empsy® Network (www.empsy.com), the principal author of *The Psychology of Coaching, Mentoring & Learning*, and a senior lecturer at UEL in Coaching (http://www.uel.ac.uk).

Lynne Millward is an Occupational Psychologist with 20 years of research and evidence-based consulting experience working with individuals, teams and organisations. As a Reader in the Psychology Department at the University of Surrey, Lynne is director of the undergraduate programme, while maintaining a busy research and publishing career that has resulted in two seminal textbooks and numerous high-impact journal articles. She continues to consult both with SHM Ltd and in private practice.

Alanna O'Broin is a Coaching Psychologist, a Counselling Psychologist and a Consulting Editor of *The Coaching Psychologist*. Following a city career as a Fund Manager, she runs her own coaching practice. Her research interests include coach and coachee contributions to the coaching relationship and coaching outcome.

Christine Oliver is Course Leader for the MSc in Systemic Management, Coaching and Consultation for the Institute of Family Therapy, London; Course Leader for the MSc in Systemic Psychotherapy at Kensington Consultation Centre, London; and a Consultant Family Therapist in the Department of Psychotherapy, St. Bartholemew's Hospital, London. She also works independently as an Organisational Consultant and Systemic Psychotherapist working to facilitate individual and organisational change. She is Co-Founder, with Beverly Clarke, of Business Therapy, providing coaching for individuals, teams and organisations. She provides training and consultancy for a number of organisations in the UK as well as working internationally. A primary interest is in consultancy methodologies for structuring dialogue to engender reflexive organisational development. She is co-author of *Complexity, Relationships and Strange Loops:*

A Reflexive Practice Guide (2003) and author of *Reflexive Inquiry* (2005).

Philippe Rosinski is a world authority in executive coaching, team coaching and global leadership development. He is the first European to have been designated Master Certified Coach by the International Coach Federation. He has pioneered a global approach to coaching and the Harvard Business School chose his groundbreaking book *Coaching Across Cultures* as its featured book recommendation for business leaders. He is Principal of Rosinski & Company (www.philrosinski.com), an international network organisation that helps leaders, teams and organisations unleash their human potential to achieve sustainable high performance. He is a Professor in the MBA programme for global managers at the Kenichi Ohmae Graduate School of Business in Tokyo, Japan. He holds a Master of Science from Stanford University, California.

Gil Schwenk co-leads Bath Consultancy Group's Coaching Excellence and Supervision capability. He is an executive coach and specialises in enabling organisations to create their coaching culture and harvest systemic feedback from coaching. He has trained hundreds of coaches and mentors in a wide range of private and public organisations. He is also an executive coach on executive development programmes at London Business School. Gil is on the board of the European Mentoring and Coaching Council UK (EMCC) and represents EMCC on the 'roundtable' of UK coaching bodies. As the former Chair of Standards, he led the creation of professional standards for the UK and Europe. He is also the co-author of *Coaching Supervision: Maximising the Potential of Coaching*, which was published by the Chartered Institute of Personnel and Development in 2006.

Chris Smewing is an Occupational Psychologist and Chartered member of the Institute of Personnel and Development. He combines a strong academic background with extensive practical experience of working as a human resources specialist and business psychology consultant. His main areas of focus are individual assessment and coaching, leadership development and the facilitation of change. He works with teams and individuals to help them recognise and develop their skills and contribution to the organisation. He has worked with many types of organisations, in both the private and the public sector, across Europe and Asia.

Peter Welman has worked as a careers counsellor and is now a practising coach and therapist. He has a particular interest in the efficacy of anarchy in helping relations.

Preface

Coaching and coaching psychology within their own domains have become professions (Palmer, 2008a). They both have national and international professional bodies providing their members with codes of ethics and practice, supervision recommended for practitioners, national and international registers of practitioners, accreditation and certification of courses and practitioners, professional qualifications such as membership grades, university or exam board accredited courses, peer-reviewed academic and practitioner journals abstracted in psychological databases such as psycINFO, and in some countries such as the United Kingdom, they have National Occupational Standards developed by national training organisations (Palmer, 2008a, 2008b). Of course, it could be argued that in some countries coaching is still viewed as an industry as not all the criteria for a profession are fulfilled.

Coaching and coaching psychology have an increasing number of models and approaches, many underpinned by both theory and research. The professional coach or psychologist is expected to increase their knowledge and enhance their competencies through continuing professional development and education. Yet, over the past decade it has become clear that the coaching relationship so often referred to in passing in the coaching and coaching psychology literature and also by practitioners has been based on limited research. If based on any research at all, then assumptions are sometimes extrapolated from psychotherapist–client or sports coaching–athlete relationships. In this book we have

focused on different aspects of the coach–coachee relationship informed by relevant theory and research. To provide
an overall picture of coaching relationships we have also
included a chapter on the interpersonal relationship in the
training and supervision of coaches.

We hope this book will inform professional practice and
encourage more practitioners and researchers to reflect on
what we know, what we do not know and what we need to find
out about the coach–coachee relationship. Finally, we would
like to thank our authors for their excellent contributions.

Stephen Palmer
Almuth McDowall
1 June 2009

References

Palmer, S. (2008a) How you can personally contribute to the field of
coaching. Paper presented at the Association for Coaching,
Embracing Excellence, International Conference, London,
March.
Palmer, S. (2008b) Coaching psychology: the European train has
arrived so welcome aboard. But will it leave the station on time
and where is it going? Keynote paper presented at the 1st
European Coaching Psychology Conference, London, December.

Foreword

As far back as AD 121, The Roman Emperor Marcus Aurelius said that we all should do 'what's in front of you with precise and genuine seriousness, tenderly, willingly and with justice ... yes, you can – if you do everything as if it were the last thing you were doing in your life, and stop being aimless, stop letting your emotions override what your mind tells you, stop being hypocritical, self-centred, irritable. You see how few things you have to do to live a satisfying and reverent life?' His meditations were some of the first 'self-help' proclamations in history, many of which hold true today. The difference is that the pace of life has meant that fewer people have the community around them to support them during times of distress, of decision making about relationships or careers or other life style issues, as we have moved away from our extended families in search of making a living. We are more than ever before isolated and exposed to the high pressures of life, both at work and in our personal lives. We need more than ever before a surrogate for the aunties and grandmas who provided the support and guidance in our lives during the less mobile decades of the middle of the 20th century. Coaching, counselling and other psychological and facilitative approaches have developed over the last couple of decades to provide the support and 'time out' to assess our life styles, and where we should be going in each of our own personal struggles.

Coaching is a relatively new phenomenon that has had a significant and meaningful impact on the lives of many thousands of people. We see it in all walks of life, in the office, as an aid to life-style changes, as a support system for change and so on. And although there are now many books on the subject, there is little attention to the coaching relationship. This volume is unique in exploring this very important theme, and from the perspective of some of the leading academics and practitioners in the field. All the work on 'the coaching relationship' has been brought together in this one volume. This is a must-read for anybody in the field, and anybody interested in caring relationships more generally . . . you won't be disappointed.

Cary L. Cooper, CBE
Distinguished Professor of Organizational
Psychology and Health
Lancaster University Management School

The Coaching Relationship: Putting People First. An introduction

Stephen Palmer and Almuth McDowall

Introduction

There is no denying that the essence of coaching is 'putting people first'. Regardless of which techniques, frameworks or psychological underpinnings a coach might draw on, basic coaching processes all rest on interpersonal interaction in some way or another. The ultimate aims of coaching are to facilitate personal, and usually also professional, growth, learning and optimal functioning (e.g. Downey, 1999). Thus, the initial motivation is a focus on optimisation and improvement of performance as opposed to the elimination of any problems, the typical initial motive for counselling (Bachkirova, 2007). The importance of the relationship for both processes is equally high, however (Bachkirova, 2007). While there is research that provides a frame for understanding and managing the counselling relationship (we return to this issue in Chapter 3), the same is yet to be developed for coaching and coaching psychology (see O'Broin and Palmer, 2006).

This recognition of the fundamental importance of relationships in coaching provided the impetus for editing this book, which is particularly timely given the dearth of extant research on the subject and the growing importance of networks and relationships in society at large. In the following sections we provide a brief introduction to relationships in general, before linking our observations to a coaching context. The last section of this chapter provides the reader with an introduction to each of our main chapters.

Relationships and human functioning

Relationships are fundamental to human life as they ensure the survival of humankind and fulfil basic innate needs. As Maslow (1943) advocated more than six decades ago, our needs for love and belonging to others and gaining their respect need to be met (as well as having food and a roof over our heads) before we can realise our own potential (self-actualisation). While this model of human functioning has received much critique over the years from other researchers (e.g. Locke, 2000), research into such needs has recently undergone a resurgence (see Latham, 2005) as psychologists continue to seek a holistic explanation for the motivations of human behaviours.

Relationships in the modern world

Over the last two decades, the concept of 'social capital' (e.g. Field, 2008) has taken off rapidly in the social sciences. In essence, this concept proposes the simple theory that relationships and networks matter. Indeed, we have witnessed a shift in how society functions. Over the last decades, we have seen 'locally embedded communities declining dramatically' (Halpern, 2004: viii), such as local neighbourhoods, which are being replaced by different types of communities. Some of these have of course been facilitated by modern web technology. The success of social networking sites such as Facebook and Friends Reunited has made it easy to get in touch with existing or old friends and acquaintances and find new ones through rapidly grown networks. Social e-networks are also growing in importance in the business world, where business connections are made and vacancies advertised through online networks such as LinkedIn. However, writers such as Harkin (2009) argue that instead of bringing relationships closer, these new developments have contributed to social alienation and to huge amounts of productive time being wasted.

Given that networking through relationships is so essential to how society works, to what extent do we experience functional and healthy relationships? The evidence would suggest that patterns of relationships have certainly changed. In the UK, we are less likely to marry than we ever were (National Statistics). At the same time the demand for relationship counselling has soared with the advent of the global economic downturn (Penell, 2009). This is not to say that we have given up our faith in and need for personal relationships. For instance, we have witnessed an increase in 'patchwork families' over the last decade, where children might be jointly brought up by divorced parents for instance, each of whom might have a new partner who may also bring children from a previous relationship to the set-up. So while we intuitively might still assume that relationships are linear and have a distinct start and end, the reality may not reflect this assumption, as we may move in and out of relationships depending on our circumstances at the time.

Professional relationships

What about relationships in professional or work domains? It has long been argued that the 'psychological contract' has changed, as long-term employment relationships marked by very clear boundaries and contractual arrangements are in decline, and more short-term employment relationships, often involving 'portfolio workers' who negotiate their terms and conditions on a contract-by-contract basis, have become the norm (e.g. Rousseau, 1996). Stephen Taylor (2002) has presented research that showed that most people resign from their job because they are 'sick of their immediate boss', pointing to the fact that good relationships are key to retention and engagement in the workplace, Taylor saying that 'the difficult bit [at work] is the area of interpersonal relationships'.

Implications for coaching and coaching psychology practice

The above observations have implications for coaching practice. First, the increasing recognition that relationships are important is likely to contribute to the continued growth of coaching in the workplace, which frequently tackles issues arising from other interpersonal aspects within the confines of a two-way coach–coachee relationship. Thus, as others have also recognised (de Haan, 2008), relationships are at the heart of coaching. Not only is the content of coaching sessions frequently in some way concerned with relationships, the process itself is always based on relationships. These necessarily involve the coach, the coachee, but often also a client (commissioning organisation). Moreover, coaching may also involve others directly, such as a line manager who may be party to any outcomes, or indirectly through coaching techniques such as circular questioning.

In addition, we recognise that while some coaching relationships have a very clear timeframe, goal and purpose, there are other coaching scenarios that do not fit into this bracket. From our own experience we can, for instance, think of examples where a coachee had first been seen in his or her teens, and then came back to the coach for career coaching advice several years later, embarked on their chosen career and then sought the coach's services again at a later stage. This complexity provides the rationale for the present book, as the nonlinearity of relationships, the often complicated interpersonal dynamics and potential confidentiality issues need to be considered in a proactive rather than reactive way in coaching. We have deliberately taken an edited approach, where we have asked contributors who are all knowledgeable in particular fields to contribute particular chapters. While we recognise that this book cannot cover everything, we have carefully chosen a range of topics to assist coaches to build their own framework for understanding and managing relationships in coaching.

Introduction to *The Coaching Relationship: Putting People First*

Whereas most coaching books focus on particular models and approaches or different types of coaching such as personal or executive coaching, this book focuses on different interpersonal aspects of the coach–coachee relationship. In

Chapter 2, Alanna O'Broin and Stephen Palmer introduce an interpersonal perspective on the coaching relationship. They take themes from relationship science, which resonate with themes from the coaching and coaching psychology literature, and demonstrate how the coaching relationship can be seen as unique. They emphasise the actions and properties of both coachee and coach in the whole coaching process. In Chapter 3 they build on the previous chapter's introduction to an interpersonal perspective on the coaching relationship. They spotlight five further topics that are important to the coaching relationship such as the psychological contract in coaching, and coach–coachee matching, and also consider the relevance of game theory to executive and business coaching.

In Chapter 4, Almuth McDowall and Lynne Millward focus on feeding back, feeding forward and setting goals. The chapter looks at feedback in terms of both process and content, with a particular focus on both the role of interpersonal relationships and potential outcomes, such as performance and mood. They draw on diverse theoretical interventions including Control Theory (Carver and Scheier, 1981) and Regulatory Focus Theory (Higgins, 1997). In Chapter 5, Chris Smewing and Almuth McDowall discuss assessment in coaching. They outline different types of assessment, concentrating on the workplace, and discuss the results of a survey investigating the current usage of different assessment instruments in a coaching context. Importantly, they consider the circumstances when assessment instruments should or should not be used.

In Chapter 6, Christine Oliver considers reflexive coaching: linking meaning and action in the leadership system. She takes a systemic approach to the coaching relationship and task. She outlines the relevance of a systemic orientation, a framework for understanding and methodological tools and then applies them to a case study where an executive struggled with a leadership challenge. In Chapter 7, Lina Daouk-Öyry and Philippe Rosinski investigate coaching across cultures. They define culture and coaching from a multinational perspective and recognise that coaches are increasingly facing a new challenge in their practice – the influence of culture (St Claire-Ostwald, 2007). Using examples and case studies, they explore the ways in which individuals can differ through the Cultural Orientations Framework (COF™) (Rosinski, 2003).

In Chapter 8, Peter Welman and Tatiana Bachkirova consider the issue of power in the coaching relationship. They identify the form of power that is an issue and compare it with related concepts. Then they explore why coaches need to pay attention to this phenomenon. The chapter ends with a list of useful recommendations for coaches. In Chapter 9, Elaine Cox looks at ending well in the coaching relationship. She notes that two of the main reasons why coaches desire a good ending to their work are to provide customer satisfaction and gain repeat business. The key aim of the chapter is to explore how a beneficial ending to the coaching alliance can be achieved and the significance of the contracting process is also highlighted.

In Chapter 10, Ho Law covers coaching relationships and ethical practice. He believes that there is a noticeable absence of the topic of ethics in conversation among coaches and coachees. He argues that coaches may need more practical information about ethics in coaching, which he covers in the chapter. He concludes that ethical coaching can improve trust in relationships between coach and coachees, individuals and groups, and can also strengthen the coherence of the ethical culture within the coaching profession and its clients' organisations. In Chapter 11, Peter Hawkins and Gil Schwenk focus on the interpersonal relationship in the training and supervision of coaches. They explore the centrality of interpersonal relationships to coaching, coach training and supervision. They introduce and expand on the CLEAR model of coaching and the seven-eyed model of supervision, both of which emphasise the importance of interpersonal relationships in the training and supervision of effective coaches.

Each chapter includes a list of references, a list of recommended books and reflective questions for further reflection or discussion within teaching settings. The book concludes with final reflections from the editors, a glossary and web resources.

Reflective questions

- Is there a real need for coaches and coaching psychologists to reflect on the relationship in coaching?
- Why has the coaching relationship been under-researched?
- In your opinion, to achieve effective coaching, what is more important: the coach–coachee relationship, coaching models or coaching techniques?

References

Bachkirova, T. (2007) Role of coaching psychology in defining boundaries between counselling and coaching. In S. Palmer and A. Whybrow (eds) *Handbook of Coaching Psychology: A Guide for Practitioners*. London: Routledge.

Carver, C. and Scheier, M. (1981) *Attention and Self-regulation: A Control Theory Approach to Human Behavior*. New York: Springer.

De Haan, E. (2008) *Relational Coaching: Journeys Towards Mastering One-to-One Learning*. Chichester: John Wiley & Sons.

Downey, M. (1999) *Effective Coaching*. London: Orion.

Field, J. (2008) *Social Capital*. London: Routledge.

Halpern, D. (2004) *Social Capital*. Cambridge: Polity Press.

Harkin, J. (2009) *Cyburbia*. London: Little, Brown.

Higgins, E.T. (1997) Beyond pleasure and pain. *American Psychologist*, 52: 1280–1300.

Latham, G. (2005) *Work Motivation: History, Theory, Research and Practice*. London: Sage.

Locke, E.A. (2000) Motivation, cognition and action: an analysis of studies of task goals and knowledge. *Applied Psychology: An International Review*, 49: 408–429.

Maslow, A.H. (1943) A theory of human motivation. *Psychological Review*, 50: 370–396.

National Statistics. First Marriages: Age and Sex (England and Wales): Population Trends 133. Retrieved from http://www.statistics.gov.uk/STATBASE/ssdataset.asp?vlnk=9554 on 24 March 2009.

O'Broin, A. and Palmer, S. (2006) Reappraising the coach–client relationship. In S. Palmer and A. Whybrow (eds) *Handbook of Coaching Psychology: A Guide for Practitioners*. London: Routledge.

Pennell, S. (2009) Money worries 'affecting couples'. BBC newschannel feature first broadcast 27 February 2009. Retrieved from http://news.bbc.co.uk/1/hi/uk/7914119.stm on 24 March 2009.

Rosinski, P. (2003) *Coaching Across Cultures*. London: Nicholas Brealey Publishing.

Rousseau, D. (1996) *Psychological Contracts in Organizations*. London: Sage.

St Claire-Ostwald, B. (2007) Carrying cultural baggage: the contribution of socio-cultural anthropology to cross-cultural coaching. *International Journal of Evidence Based Coaching and Mentoring*, 5: 45–52.

Taylor, S. (2002) *Employee Retention Handbook*. London: CIPD. Summary retrieved from www.cipd.co.uk/pressoffice/_articles/14112002175156.htm?IsSrchRes=1 on 31 March 2009.

Recommended books

De Haan, E. (2008) *Relational Coaching: Journeys Towards Mastering One-to-One Learning*. Chichester: John Wiley & Sons.

Downey, M. (1999) *Effective Coaching*. London: Orion.

Palmer, S. and Whybrow, A. (2007) *Handbook of Coaching Psychology: A Guide for Practitioners*. London: Routledge.

Stober, D.R. and Grant, A.M. (2006) *Evidence Based Coaching Handbook: Putting Best Practices to Work for Your Clients*. Hoboken, NJ: Wiley.

2

Introducing an interpersonal perspective on the coaching relationship

Alanna O'Broin and Stephen Palmer

Introduction

> . . . the self exists in a relationship context.
>
> (Reis *et al.*, 2000: 844)

In viewing the coaching relationship through the conceptual lens of an interpersonal perspective, this chapter advances a rationale for the special significance of appreciating and understanding the coaching relationship context in which the individual coachee is embedded. Implications of such an interpersonal perspective are that the actions and properties of *both* partners in the dyad determines their interpersonal reaction.[1]

This chapter briefly introduces themes from relationship science that resonate with themes from the coaching and coaching psychology literature: an increasing focus on coaching processes, a growing awareness of the vital role of the coaching relationship and increasing findings of the importance of interpersonal aspects of coaching. The differences between coaching and three other helping relationships are then discussed, and this is followed by the

---

[1] The focus of this chapter is interpersonal factors, arguably the focal feature of the context from the individual's perspective (Reis *et al.*, 2000). In a broader sense, the interaction of the dyad is also determined by the physical and social environments in which they interact, and by how all these factors interact with each other.

presentation of a perspective on how the coaching relationship can be seen as unique. Finally, the chapter summarises its conclusions in bullet point form.

The concept of relationships

Until relatively recently, study of relationships in the area of relationship science neglected conceptual issues posed by the concept of relationship (Reis *et al.*, 2000). The term 'relationship' was considered part of common language, therefore not requiring academic definition and scrutiny (Berscheid and Peplau, 1983). With recognition of the wide variety of meanings, not only of the term relationship, but also of referents of the term, this has changed, and researchers now concur that *interactions* between the partners of a relationship are its essence, and that *mutual influence* is the hallmark of such interactions (Kelley *et al.*, 1983; Berscheid and Reis, 1998; Reis, 2007). There is recognition that social interaction is necessary although insufficient for a relationship to exist, particularly in the case of close relationships where strong mutual influence of each others' behaviour over time, as well as more affect than less close relationships, is evident. Findings from evolutionary psychology and social psychology of the importance of social groups and interactions also assert that relationship context may be a more important determinant of behaviour than previously supposed (Reis *et al.*, 2000).

Themes from the coaching and coaching psychology literature

If interactions between partners, mutual influence between close relationship partners, and the relationship context are key in broader relationships, what of the coaching and coaching relationship? Three themes from the coaching and coaching psychology literature can help inform our interpersonal perspective on the coaching relationship and these echo the themes from the broader relationship science literature. The themes are an increasing focus in the literature on coaching processes, growing awareness of the vital role of the coaching relationship and greater recognition of the importance of the interpersonal aspects of coaching.

An increasing focus on coaching processes

Kilburg (2004) highlighted a potential parallel between the Dodoville conjecture in psychotherapy outcome research where, after much research time and effort over decades, different conceptual approaches were found to be broadly equivalent in outcome effectiveness (Luborsky, 1995), and research findings in the coaching literature of common effects, regardless of conceptual foundations espoused by coaching practitioners.

Since this time, the coaching context has witnessed a trend from research and discussion largely based on broad comparisons of different conceptual frameworks of coaching towards increasing concentration on and calls for:

* a more pluralistic and inclusive empirical grounding for coaching research (Lowman, 2005; Stober and Grant, 2006);
* a framework of practice to enable clarity on the purpose of coaching to enable evaluation of the effectiveness of coaching to take place (Fillery-Travis and Lane, 2006, 2007);
* an in-depth investigation into the nature and complexity of multiple coaching processes, including the dynamics of the coaching relationship and the role of the self of the coach in the process (Bachkirova, 2007).

Current coaching psychology models, such as the *Contextual Coaching Model*, emphasising the processes and 'how' of coaching, are synergistic with this approach, rather than solely comparing the effectiveness of coaching models with each other (Stober and Grant, 2006). With this move towards a finer-grain investigation of coaching processes, references are increasingly being made in the literature to a more complex perspective on the interpersonal aspects of the relationship, at multiple levels of investigation, for instance in highlighting mindfulness, and meta skills of the coach (Waring, 2008).

However, as Cavanagh and Grant (2006) note, the coaching relationship, as a *'complex adaptive system'* with unpredictable next steps, and with the impossibility of prescribing interventions at a micro level, may be more accessible to an *evidence-based approach* than the traditional hypothetico-deductive model of the scientist-practitioner employing deterministic linear causality.

The vital role of the coaching relationship

Perhaps in part reflecting the lack of consensus on the definition of the term 'executive coaching' even in recent literature (Gregory *et al.*, 2008; Sperry, 2008), it is noteworthy that there exists in the coaching and coaching psychology literature a range of usages of the term 'coaching relationship'. However, as is the case with relationships more generally, the coaching relationship is considered an extremely important factor in the coaching process (Kampa-Kokesh and Anderson, 2001; O'Broin and Palmer, 2006a) and the coaching outcome (McGovern *et al.*, 2001; Gyllensten and Palmer, 2007). The coaching and coaching psychology literature repeatedly attests to the need to establish and maintain a meaningful relationship between coachee and coach (Wasylyshyn, 2003; Bluckert, 2005a; Stober and Grant, 2006; O'Broin and Palmer, 2007; Kemp, 2008), while the research literature database on the coaching relationship remains at a relatively early stage in its development.

Increasing evidence of the role of interpersonal aspects

With a greater focus on the processes of coaching has come increasing evidence of the importance of interpersonal, or relational, aspects of coaching. In the coaching and coaching psychology literature, trust figures repeatedly as an important indicator of the quality of the coaching relationship and has been hypothesised as a factor that may contribute to the effectiveness of coaching (Lowman, 2007). Luebbe (2005), for instance, in a study investigating effective outcomes from executive coaching with coaches, coachees and human resource brokers, found that trust was the highest-rated coaching attribute, of primary importance to all three groups. Luebbe concluded that this finding signalled the primacy of the relational aspects of coaching and their necessity for moving forward with later interventions. Trust and mutual respect were similarly found to be of fundamental importance in coaching high achievers (Jones and Spooner, 2006) and necessary for a relationship of trust in a review of themes from coaching in multicultural contexts (Lowman, 2007).

This theme of the importance of interpersonal aspects of coaching is further supported by de Haan (2008) and de Haan *et al.* (2008), who found in a study of the helpfulness of coaching with executive coachees that the crucial predictor of the outcome of coaching was the coaching relationship as perceived by the *coachee*, rather than specific coach behaviours. Coachees were also found to value most those coach qualities beneficial to the coaching relationship, such as listening, understanding and encouragement. Those coachees who attributed coach qualities such as being friendly, courteous, attentive and responsive experienced significantly better outcomes.

Summary

In this introductory discussion on the interpersonal aspects of the coaching relationship, the broader themes from relationship science of the importance of interactions between partners, mutual influence between close relationship partners, and the relationship context have been reflected in the themes arising from the coaching and coaching psychology literature.

We have highlighted a call in the coaching and coaching psychology literature for better explanations for coaching processes, in tandem with repeated statements of the importance of the coaching relationship to coaching and coaching psychology outcomes and an increasing recognition of the importance of interpersonal aspects of the coaching relationship. Declaring the importance of the coaching relationship and other phenomena in the coaching process takes us only so far. The emphasis going forward will be on demonstrating empirically why and how the coaching relationship and, in the broader picture, other factors, both individually and in combination, contribute to the coaching process and to coaching outcome. This task holds certain challenges:

- the need to develop theories, as far as this discussion is concerned, on the relationship between coach and coachee, and in the broader context, on individual developmental change in the organisational context (see also Bachkirova, 2007) and to establish empirical findings;
- the need to seek, along with outcome, understanding of underlying mechanisms, context, and moderators in the processes guiding the coaching relationship;
- in asking more sophisticated questions at an intermediate level of detail, the requirement for developing research methodology capable of undertaking evidence-based research at this level of complexity.

Is the coaching relationship different?

Helping relationships

In order to extrapolate whether and how the coaching relationship differs from other helping relationships, a comparison will now be made between the coaching relationship and three 'helping' relationships – counselling, sport psychology and friendship. This comparison begins with a recognition of the similarities between the four relationships.

If relationship science emphasises the interactions, mutual influence and context of relationships more generally, how are helping relationships characterised? Egan (2002), in noting the consensus in the counselling and psychotherapy outcome literature on the importance of the relationship between client and helper, highlights the significant differences in how the relationship is seen to be characterised and played out:

- *The relationship itself*: The relationship is central to the therapy process, which is seen as an interpersonal relationship, not just involving an interpersonal relationship.

- *The relationship as a means to an end*: The relationship is a practical means of enabling the client and counsellor to do the work required by whatever process is used and for the client to manage a particular problem better.
- *The relationship and outcomes*: The relationship is often a time-limited, pragmatic approach focusing on what the client needs to do straight away to find solutions to their issues.

Coaching as a helping relationship

Coaching is a helping relationship (Renner, 2007). Helping is foremost a common cross-cultural human experience. Often such helping takes place within a formal profession, such as coaching, sport psychology or counselling. Helping may also take place when a second set of professional helpers helps others at times of distress, such as doctors, lawyers, nurses or teachers; or alternatively when any person tries to help another, such as family, friends or acquaintances (Egan, 2002).

People seek help from formal helpers either due to problem situations that they are currently unable to handle (Lampropoulos, 2001), or due to missed opportunities or unused potential, or both (Egan, 2002). Egan (2002) highlights two principal goals of helping:

- helping people manage their problems in living more effectively and developing unused resources and missed opportunities more fully;
- helping people improve at helping themselves in their everyday lives.

In a broad comparison, all four of our relationships – coaching, sport psychology, counselling and friendship – can be categorised as 'helping' relationships (although helping is one facet of friendship, and friendship may occur without helping taking place). If these relationships are similar as 'helping relationships', how else can they be differentiated?

Simple distinctions

First, there are differences in the characteristics of friendship, compared with the other three relationships. The primary one is that friendship is characterised by its voluntary nature (Bukowski and Sippola, 2005), unlike the other three, professional relationships. This differentiation obviously brings with it issues of competences, ethics and confidentiality in professional relationships, which do not occur formally in friendship. Friendship research also documents that *equality* as a characteristic of friendship dyads facilitates relational satisfaction (Neff and Harter, 2003) is associated with self-disclosure (Veniegas and Peplau, 1997) and, arguably, facilitates open communication (Ueno and Adams, 2008).

The context of sport and exercise has been highlighted as a differentiator of sport psychology from other activities (Brown, 2001), with different emphases arising from this difference, such as a focus on motor learning and psychophysiological processes to maximise fitness and consistent movement (Collins, 2008), as well as the potential for a coach–athlete relationship of emotional intensity and possibly greater longevity than would be usual in coaching (O'Broin and Palmer, 2006b).

Comparisons of coaching and counselling/psychotherapy have been prominent in the coaching and coaching psychology literature. Those findings salient to this discussion centre around the different use of the coach's self as a vehicle for change (Hart *et al.*, 2001), the different presence that the coach brings to the coaching relationship and the different intentions of the coaching and counselling processes (Bluckert, 2005b).

Executive coaching can be differentiated from the other three helping relationships by citing the frequent three-way involvement of the organisation in the relationship, although workplace counselling also features the impact of the organisation not only on the administrative dimension, but also on the interpersonal dimension (Carroll, 1999). Executive coaching differs from workplace counselling in this respect as it usually attempts to align the goals of the coachee with those of the organisation.

A further attempt to find the differences

Bachkirova (2007), in reviewing the boundaries between coaching and counselling, concluded that attempts in the literature to define the purpose or end result of each activity at a higher level of generalisation and describe how the end result is achieved in greater detail have helped. However, they have their limitations. Bachkirova (2007) compared and contrasted coaching and counselling using alternative aspects, this time hoping to avoid the pitfalls of the first two attempts and noting that those similarities found between coaching and counselling were important factors in contributing to the effectiveness of coaching and counselling. These similarities were:

- the importance of the relationship between the two participants;
- the role of the practitioner's self;
- the commitment of the client.

If we now add sport psychology and friendship to the table for comparison, we can see that at this high level of abstraction, the four helping relationships appear similar on these three aspects (see Table 2.1).

It is when we include the remaining aspects from Table 2.1, as well as the additional aspects of the status of the relationship, level of self-disclosure and level and type of affect for the four helping relationships that we begin to see some differences across the four relationships, even at this high level of generalisation.

The level of self-disclosure in the four relationships tends to range from low, in the case of counselling, moderate in coaching and sport psychology to high in friendship, although this will vary depending on the individuals, the situation and the context. With regard to the type and level of affect, while the professional helper may or may not 'like' their coachee, athlete or client, or *vice versa*, there needs to be a work-potentiating bond in order for the work of the coaching, counselling or sports coaching to take place (see Chapter 3 for further discussion of this topic). In friendship, on the other hand, in order to help a friend, particularly in

Table 2.1 Comparison of important aspects across coaching and three other helping relationships

	Coaching	Counselling	Sport psychology	Friendship
Aspects contributing to the effectiveness of the helping process				
Importance of relationship in process	High	High	High	High
Role of helper's self in process	Very important	Very important	Very important	Very important
Importance of commitment of the helped	High	High	High	High
Additional important aspects of helping relationships				
Level of self-disclosure	Moderate	Low	Moderate	High
Level and type of affect	Work-potentiating bond	Work-potentiating bond	Work-potentiating bond	Liking, broad affective bond
Status of relationship	Professional	Professional	Professional	Non-professional
Ultimate purpose and benefit	Development and well-being of individual (if sponsored – also benefit of organisation)	Development and well-being of individual	Preparation for athletic success, optimum performance and well-being of individual	Well-being of individual
Initial motivation	Enhancing life, improving performance	Eliminating psychological problem and dysfunctions	Optimising and maintaining physical excellence and performance	Problem-solving, social support

Context of interventions	Specified by the contract, according to the client's goal, the coach's area of expertise and the assignment of a sponsor if involved	Open to any and potentially all areas of client's life	Specified by the contract, according to the athlete's goal or goals	Open to any and potentially all areas of friend's life
Expectations for change	From relative satisfaction to much higher satisfaction	From high dissatisfaction to reasonable satisfaction	From relative or high satisfaction to much higher satisfaction	From dissatisfaction to reasonable satisfaction
Possible outcome	Attainment of goals, increased well-being and productivity	Increased well-being, unexpected positive changes in various areas of life	Attainment of performance goals, increased well-being and fitness	Increased well-being
Theoretical foundation	May include psychology, education, sociology, philosophy, management, health and social care, etc.	Psychology and philosophy	Psychology, psycho-physiology	Personal philosophy and values
Main professional skills of helper	Listening, questioning, feedback, explicit goal setting and action planning	Listening, questioning, feedback, use of tools and methods specific to particular approaches	Listening, questioning, feedback, explicit goal setting and action planning	n/a

Source: Adapted from Bachkirova (2007) and extended.

terms of an ongoing helping activity, there arguably needs to be sufficient liking or an affective bond to be present. The professional/non-professional distinction has already been noted in the section on helping relationships.

In terms of ultimate purpose and benefit, there appears to be some overlap across the four relationships. On initial motivation, there are a range of motivations, with counselling, friendship, coaching and sport psychology placed on a scale from eliminating distress and psychological problems, to optimising excellence, with coaching and sport psychology at the end of the spectrum most likely to be stimulated by organisations to increase performance/excellence, friendship more likely to be an exploration to improve well-being, and counselling likely to be either the same or a wish to eliminate psychological distress. The context of interventions is likely to be narrower in coaching and sport psychology where the coachee and athlete respectively may be constrained by the organisational need or sporting context concerned. The theoretical foundation aspect could be declared absent in friendship, although the friend's personal philosophy and values may serendipitously emulate some aspects of theoretical approaches. Finally, in expectations for change there is overlap in the dimensions, although the four relationships could be ranged broadly from counselling, friendship, coaching to sport psychology, on a scale ranging from dissatisfaction to higher satisfaction.

Summary

In discussing the differences between the coaching relationship and the therapeutic, the coach–athlete and friendship relationships, their degree of overlap was noted – they can all be construed as 'helping' relationships.

In considering differences in the purpose of the relationships at a broad level of generalisation, coaching was differentiated from friendship in being a professional rather than a voluntary relationship, in having a different context from the other three relationships, in using the self and presence of the coach differently as a vehicle for change and in noting the three-way involvement of coach, coachee and client organisation often present in the coaching relationship (in combination with aligning the goals of coaching with those of the organisation) creating a different relationship.

Finally, in comparing the important aspects contributing to the effectiveness of each particular process, as well as other aspects identified by Bachkirova (2007) as important, across the additional coach–athlete and friendship relationships, at a high level of generalisation, for all four relationships the importance of the relationship in the process and the importance of the commitment of the person helped was high, with the role of the helper's self in the process being very important.

Across additional aspects, some differences between coaching and the other relationships became apparent, although these were mainly in terms of degree, and again there were some overlaps. The main differences were in the initial motivation of coaching, and the expectations for change in coaching, compared with the other three relationships, as well as a perhaps broader theoretical foundation in coaching, from across the wider behavioural science literature (Cavanagh and Grant, 2006).

What is unique to the coaching relationship?

Having discussed the differences between coaching and three other relationships, let's now consider what is unique about the coaching relationship.

Unique commonalities

Haugh and Paul's (2008) use of the phrase 'unique commonalities' alludes to the idiosyncratic aspect of every relationship as a meeting of two unique individuals, while recognising the 'common factors' or core conditions necessary but not necessarily sufficient for change in a helping relationship. Kemp (2008: 32) echoes this sentiment in describing the coaching relationship as 'a directionally influential helping dynamic that is established between two unique psychological entities'. While at this level every relationship is unique, we can look further in conceptualising the coaching relationship as a unique relationship. If we now move from the macro-level comparison in Table 2.1, to a meso- or intermediate-level examination of one of the factors contributing to the effectiveness of coaching – the coach's use of self – we can illustrate a perspective on how the coaching relationship is unique. To this end, we will focus on an example of the coach's self-reflection and response process during the engagement stage of the relationship, moving from a discussion of the process at the macro level, through to illustration at the meso level using a vignette, and at the micro level using examples of coach–coachee dialogue deriving from the vignette.

The coach's use of self

This *meso-level* perspective (see Figure 2.1) positions its focus at a finer degree of specification than the higher degree of generalisation usually addressed in the coaching research literature, in this instance at the level of interpersonal process elements during the engagement stage of

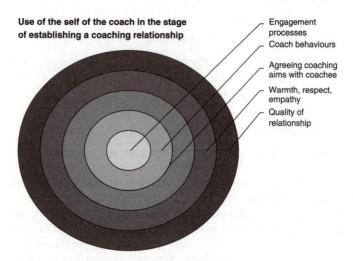

Figure 2.1 Establishing a coaching relationship

(adapted from Hardy *et al.*, 2007)

the relationship. As has already been discussed for all four relationships above, in coaching:

- the relationship is important;
- the importance of the commitment of the coachee is high;
- the role of the practitioner's self in the process is very important.

In addition to the presence or absence of these aspects, a further vital consideration is *how* the self of the coach is used and to what purpose, in establishing and later developing and maintaining the coaching relationship, in the particular coachee's context. In the coaching relationship, how the self of the coach is used, and how the coachee responds, in an iterative process, will impact on the qualitative nature of the resulting coaching relationship.

Engagement objectives

Engagement objectives during the first stage of establishing a relationship include expectancies, intentions, motivation and hope (Hardy *et al.*, 2007). Applying these macro-level engagement objectives to the coaching context proposes that building the coachee's expectations, as well as the coach demonstrating expectancies for the usefulness of the coaching, are important for engagement of the coachee. Coachee intentions and motivation for hope also need to be developed (Green *et al.*, 2006, 2007; Pooley, 2006). Good relationship ratings (McGovern *et al.*, 2001; Wasylyshyn, 2003; de Haan, 2008) early in the relationship are likely to be associated with high levels of coachee involvement.

Coach behaviours

Coach behaviours associated with engagement objectives in this discussion include warmth, respect (Jones and Spooner, 2006) and empathy/compassion (Boyatzis *et al.*, 2006) – three of Rogers' (1957) therapeutic conditions – with empathy particularly associated with good engagement. Mutual involvement (Orenstein, 2006) and discussing and agreeing the coaching aims with the coachee are also critical to engagement.

The engagement objectives and coach behaviours outlined above are macro-level factors at a high level of generalisation. It is at the meso or intermediate level of focus that these factors display what is unique to the coaching relationship, in this instance highlighting the decision-making and self-reflection involved in the coach's use of self, tailored to a specific coachee. This meso-level focus is illustrated in the vignette below.

Vignette

James, 32 years old, has strong technical and analytical skills, and has recently been made a partner of a large firm of accountants. While he is pleased at achieving a goal that he has worked towards for several years, he is also concerned that his new position involves managing a team of six, one of whom, Martin, was previously his peer. As part of a programme initiated by his organisation to support newly appointed senior managers, James has been offered coaching. His coach is Susanna, whom he is meeting for their first coaching meeting. James confirms that he wants the focus area of the coaching to be on developing and improving appropriate communication skills with his team.

Discussion

During their discussion establishing James' specific goal, Susanna notices several points:

- While couching his comments in a humorous manner, James demonstrates a certain ambivalence to change in several statements such as 'I want to communicate differently with my team now that I am their manager, but if I do, they won't take me seriously'.
- James has a tendency to focus on the intellectual and technical aspects of his new role.
- James expresses anger towards Martin, who he believes should show respect towards him as his new manager.

Susanna's self-reflection and responses to these points in the session

- Having probed and established that James' attitude to change is not due to broader dissatisfactions with his organisation or with the rationale for coaching as a resource, Susanna hypothesises that James' ambivalence and preference for working in his 'comfort zone' of technical work indicates that he is at the contemplative stage in the change cycle (Prochaska *et al.*, 1992). She concludes that her priority is to work with open questions, reflective listening statements, and affirmations to check out her understanding and facilitate an atmosphere of acceptance, in a motivational interviewing format (Passmore and Whybrow, 2007) exploring James' ambivalence, and working collaboratively towards engagement and change.
- Recollecting James' use of humour, Susanna too uses humour in her responses, hoping to build rapport and warmth and further encourage a collaborative framework, and improved interpersonal communication in the coaching. She notices that James appears more relaxed and open in his responses as the meeting progresses.
- In exploring James' thinking, it transpires that he believes that Martin, who is extremely self-assured and popular, and who is peeved at being passed-over for promotion, 'should' fall into line now that James is his manager. A further thinking error blocking James' progress is 'If I don't manage my team and Martin effectively, I've failed'. To tackle James' thinking errors of blame and demands, and resulting unhealthy anger, Susanna notes that thinking skills could be used, within a cognitive behavioural coaching framework (Palmer and Szymanska, 2007; Neenan, 2008; Palmer, 2009) later in the coaching process.

These points provide only a snapshot of the ongoing meta-level thinking and reflecting taking place as Susanna perceives, reflects and responds to James' verbal and non-verbal indicators, within his organisational context in their coaching meeting, while monitoring and self-regulating her own attitudes

> and emotions resulting in her micro-level responses and inter-
> ventions, to which James in turn responds.

Taking Susanna's self-reflections on James' ambivalence to change from the above vignette as one example area,
the coach–coachee dialogues below display examples of how
these meso-level self-reflections are translated into micro-
level responses by James and Susanna.

Reflective listening statements

JAMES: I want to communicate as a manager with my
team, but they won't take me seriously.

SUSANNA: You believe all your team members won't take
you seriously as their manager?

JAMES: Well, Martin is the main problem actually and
the others listen to him. He's done nothing but
undermine me in front of the other team members since I got the promotion and he didn't.
He needs to get real. It makes it hard for me to
manage the team and for them to take me seriously, so I've tended to keep my head down.

SUSANNA: It doesn't seem fair to you and you feel angry
about Martin's behaviour.

Here, Susanna's reflective listening statements check out
her understanding of James' ambivalence in an empathic
way. She has established that he appears willing to change;
however, his readiness to change seems to be impacted negatively by his lack of confidence that he can do so.

Assessment of James' rating of confidence in change

SUSANNA: Let's look at how confident you feel in making
this change. On a scale of 0–10, where 0 is
not confident and 10 is highly confident, how
confident do you feel about achieving your
coaching goal?

JAMES:	About . . . . . . 5, . . . yes at 5.
SUSANNA:	Why are you at 5 on the scale and not at zero?
JAMES:	Because I know I have the skills and I know what I need to achieve with the team members. It's just that Martin is sabotaging me.
SUSANNA:	So you are at 5. What would it take for you to go from 5 to 6?
JAMES:	What, other than Martin resign? (Humorously)
SUSANNA:	Yes, if Martin is here to stay!! (Laughing)
JAMES:	Well, either I need to be different in my approach, or Martin does, I suppose.

Here, Susanna has clarified that James' ambivalence to change reflects his lack of confidence to communicate differently with his team members, rather than overt communication skill deficits. The last question has also produced the first example of 'change talk' (Passmore and Whybrow, 2007: 166) in James' final response.

Summary

The coaching relationship can be considered unique, as can other relationships such as the therapeutic relationship, when evaluated from the perspective of 'unique commonalities'. However, it is when viewed from a finer, meso-level of detail, in this instance exploring how the self of the coach is used in the engagement stage of the coaching relationship, that interpersonal and contextual factors, in combination with the coach's meta-level thinking and skills, are shown to be deployed in response to the specific coachee's needs in a way unique to the coaching relationship.

Conclusions

In taking an interpersonal perspective on the coaching relationship, this chapter has emphasised the actions and properties of both coachee and coach in the coaching process. The main conclusions drawn from the discussion are provided in bullet points below:

- Rather than focusing on high-level generalisations, research studies are beginning to explore interactions and interpersonal factors within the coaching relationship in an effort to explain the coaching process.
- Developing the coaching and coaching psychology evidence base poses the dual challenges of developing explanatory theories, for instance for the relation of the coaching relationship to outcome, and devising research methodologies to measure such complex and fluid dynamics.
- Comparing the coaching relationship with three other 'helping' relationships highlighted the difficulty in making comparisons at a high level of generalisation.
- Differences of degree in the coaching relationship were identified across additional important aspects, mainly in the initial motivation of coaching, in expectations for change and in a broader theoretical foundation for coaching.
- The coaching relationship can be considered unique from the viewpoint that every relationship is unique. However, this 'unique commonality' also applies to other helping relationships.
- Use of the self of the coach at the stage of establishing a coaching relationship provided one example of how the coaching relationship can be viewed as unique.
- The requirement at the meso level for the coach to consider, negotiate and renegotiate the particular engagement objectives of the particular coachee, in their particular context, while self-reflecting and monitoring the interpersonal process between themselves and their coachee, and responding appropriately, in an iterative process over time, is one illustration of the unique nature of the coaching relationship.

Reflective questions

- The coaching relationship is a *'complex adaptive system'* with unpredictable next steps. How does this make it different from the therapeutic relationship?

- In your opinion, how unique is the coaching relationship?
- How similar are the coach–coachee, therapist–client, coach–athlete and friendship relationships?

References

Bachkirova, T. (2007) Role of coaching psychology in defining boundaries between counselling and coaching. In S. Palmer and A. Whybrow (eds) *Handbook of Coaching Psychology: A Guide for Practitioners*. London: Routledge.

Berscheid, E. and Peplau, L.A. (1983) The emerging science of close relationships. In H.H. Kelly, E. Berscheid, A. Christensen, J.H. Harvey, T.L. Huston, G. Levinger, E. McClintock, L.A. Peplau and D.R. Peterson (eds) *Close Relationships* (pp. 20–67). New York: Freeman.

Berscheid, E. and Reis, H.T. (1998) Attraction and close relationships. In D.T. Gilbert, S.T. Fiske and G. Lindzey (eds) *The Handbook of Social Psychology* (4th ed., vol. 2, pp. 193–281). New York: McGraw-Hill.

Bluckert, P. (2005a) Critical factors in executive coaching – the coaching relationship. *Industrial and Commercial Training*, 37: 336–340.

Bluckert, P. (2005b) The similarities and differences between coaching and therapy. *Industrial and Commercial Training*, 37: 91–96.

Boyatzis, R.A., Smith, M.L. and Blaize, N. (2006) Developing sustainable leaders through coaching and compassion. *Academy of Management Learning & Education*, 5: 8–24.

Brown, C.H. (2001) Clinical cross-training: compatibility of sport and family systems psychology. *Professional Psychology: Research and Practice*, 32: 19–26.

Bukowski, W.M. and Sippola, L.K. (2005) Friendship and development: putting the most human relationship in its place. *New Directions for Child and Adolescent Development*, 109: 91–98.

Carroll, M. (1999) *Workplace Counselling: A Systematic Approach to Employee Care*. London: Sage.

Cavanagh, M.J. and Grant, A.M. (2006) Coaching psychology and the scientist-practitioner model. In D.A. Lane and S. Corrie (eds) *The Modern Scientist-Practitioner: A Guide to Practice in Psychology*. London: Routledge.

Collins, D. (2008) Running the world-class programme in athletics. *The Psychologist*, 21: 682–683.

De Haan, E. (2008) *Relational Coaching: Journeys Towards Mastering One-to-One Learning*. Chichester: John Wiley & Sons.

De Haan, E., Culpin, V. and Curd, J. (2008) Executive coaching in practice: what determines helpfulness for coachees? *Consulting Psychology Journal: Practice and Research*, submitted.

Egan, G. (2002) *The Skilled Helper: A Problem-Management and Opportunity-Development Approach to Helping* (7th ed.). Pacific Grove, CA: Brooks/Cole.

Fillery-Travis, A. and Lane, D. (2006) Does coaching work or are we asking the wrong question? *International Coaching Psychology Review*, 1: 23–36.

Fillery-Travis, A. and Lane, D. (2007) Research: does coaching work? In S. Palmer and A. Whybrow (eds) *Handbook of Coaching Psychology: A Guide for Practitioners*. London: Routledge.

Green, L.S., Oades, L.G. and Grant, A.M. (2006) Cognitive-behavioural, solution-focused life coaching: enhancing goal striving, well-being and hope. *Journal of Positive Psychology*, 1: 142–149.

Green, S., Grant, A. and Rynsaardt, J. (2007) Evidence-based life coaching for senior high school students: building hardiness and hope. *International Coaching Psychology Review*, 2: 24–32.

Gregory, J.B., Levy, P.E. and Jeffers, M. (2008) Development of a model of the feedback process within executive coaching. *Consulting Psychology Journal: Practice and Research*, 60: 42–56.

Gyllensten, K. and Palmer, S. (2007) The coaching relationship: an interpretative phenomenological analysis. *International Coaching Psychology Review*, 2: 168–177.

Hardy, G., Cahill, J. and Barkham, M. (2007) Active ingredients of the therapeutic relationship that promote client change: a research perspective. In P. Gilbert and R.L. Leahy (eds) *The Therapeutic Relationship in the Cognitive Behavioral Psychotherapies*. London: Routledge.

Hart, V., Blattner, J. and Leipsic, S. (2001) Coaching versus therapy: a perspective. *Consulting Psychology Journal: Practice and Research*, 53: 229–237.

Haugh, S. and Paul, S. (2008) Conclusion: is the relationship the therapy? In S. Haugh and S. Paul (eds) *The Therapeutic Relationship: Perspective and Themes*. Ross-on-Wye: PCCS Books.

Jones, G. and Spooner, K. (2006) Coaching high achievers. *Consulting Psychology Journal: Practice and Research*, 58: 40–50.

Kampa-Kokesh, S. and Anderson, M.Z. (2001) Executive coaching: a comprehensive review of the literature. *Consulting Psychology Journal: Practice and Research*, 53: 205–228.

Kelley, H.H., Berscheid, E., Christensen, A., Harvey, J.H., Huston, T.L., Levinger, G., McClintock, E., Peplau, L.A. and Peterson, D.R. (1983) *Close Relationships*. New York: Freeman.

Kemp, T. (2008) Self-management and the coaching relationship:

exploring the coaching impact beyond models and methods. *International Coaching Psychology Review*, 3: 32–42.

Kilburg, R.R. (2004) Trudging towards Dodoville: conceptual approaches and case studies in executive coaching. *Consulting Psychology Journal: Practice and Research*, 56: 203–213.

Lampropoulos, G.K. (2001) Common processes of change in psychotherapy and seven other social interactions. *British Journal of Guidance and Counselling*, 29: 21–33.

Lowman, R.L. (2005) Executive coaching: the road to Dodoville needs paving with more than good intentions. *Consulting Psychology Journal: Practice and Research*, 57: 90–96.

Lowman, R.L. (2007) Coaching and consulting in multicultural contexts: integrating themes and issues. *Consulting Psychology Journal: Practice and Research*, 59: 296–303.

Luborsky, L. (1995) Are common factors across different psychotherapies the main explanation for the dodo bird verdict that 'Everyone has won so all shall have prizes?'. *Clinical Psychology: Science and Practice*, 2: 106–109.

Luebbe, D.M. (2005) *The Three-Way Mirror of Executive Coaching*. Dissertation Abstracts International: Section B: The Sciences and Engineering, 66(3B) 1771. Ann Arbor, MI: Proquest.

McGovern, J., Lindmann, M., Vergara, M., Murphy, S., Barker, L. and Warrenfeltz, R. (2001) Maximising the impact of executive coaching. *Manchester Review*, 6: 1–9.

Neenan, M. (2008) From cognitive behaviour therapy (CBT) to cognitive behaviour coaching (CBC). *Journal of Rational-Emotive Cognitive-Behaviour Therapy*, 26: 3–15.

Neff, K.D. and Harter, S. (2003) Relationship styles of self-focused autonomy, other-focused connectedness, and mutuality across multiple relationship contexts. *Journal of Social and Personal Relationships*, 20: 81–99.

O'Broin, A. and Palmer, S. (2006a) The coach–client relationship and contributions made by the coach in improving coaching outcome. *The Coaching Psychologist*, 2: 16–20.

O'Broin, A. and Palmer, S. (2006b) Win-win situation? Learning from parallels and differences between coaching psychology and sport psychology. *The Coaching Psychologist*, 2: 17–23.

O'Broin, A. and Palmer, S. (2007) Re-appraising the coach–client relationship: the unassuming change agent in coaching. In S. Palmer and A. Whybrow (eds) *Handbook of Coaching Psychology: A Guide for Practitioners*. London: Routledge.

Orenstein, R.L. (2006) Measuring executive coaching efficacy? The answer was right here all the time. *Consulting Psychology Journal: Practice and Research*, 58: 106–116.

Palmer, S. (2009) Rational coaching: a cognitive behavioural approach. *The Coaching Psychologist*, 5: 12–18.

Palmer, S. and Szymanska, K. (2007) Cognitive behavioural coaching: an integrative approach. In S. Palmer and A. Whybrow (eds) *Handbook of Coaching Psychology: A Guide for Practitioners*. London: Routledge.

Passmore, J. and Whybrow, A. (2007) Motivational interviewing: a specific approach for coaching psychologists. In S. Palmer and A. Whybrow (eds) *Handbook of Coaching Psychology: A Guide for Practitioners*. London: Routledge.

Pooley, J. (2006) Layers of meaning: a coaching journey. In H. Brunning (ed.) *Executive Coaching: Systems-Psychodynamic Perspective*. London: Karnac.

Prochaska, J.O., DiClemente, C.C. and Norcross, J.C. (1992) In search of how people change: applications to addictive behaviours. *American Psychologist*, 47: 1102–1114.

Reis, H. (2007) Steps toward the ripening of relationship science. *Personal Relationships*, 14: 1–23.

Reis, H.T., Collins, W.A. and Berscheid, E. (2000) The relationship context of human behavior and development. *Psychological Bulletin*, 126: 844–872.

Renner, J. (2007) Coaching abroad: insights about assets. *Consulting Psychology Journal: Practice and Research*, 59: 271–285.

Rogers, C.R. (1957) The necessary and sufficient conditions of therapeutic personality change. *Journal of Consulting Psychology*, 22: 95–103.

Sperry, L. (2008) Executive coaching: an intervention, role function, or profession? *Consulting Psychology Journal: Practice and Research*, 60: 33–37.

Stober, D.R. and Grant, A.M. (2006) Toward a contextual approach to coaching models. In D.R. Stober and A.M. Grant (eds) *Evidence Based Coaching Handbook: Putting Best Practices to Work for Your Clients*. Hoboken, NJ: Wiley.

Ueno, K. and Adams, R.G. (2008) Adult friendship: a decade review. In P. Noller and J. A. Feeney (eds) *Close Relationships: Functions, Forms and Processes*. New York: Psychology Press.

Veniegas, R.C. and Peplau, L.A. (1997) Power and the quality of same-sex friendships. *Psychology of Women Quarterly*, 21: 279–297.

Waring, P.A. (2008) Coaching the brain. *The Coaching Psychologist*, 4: 63–70.

Wasylyshyn, K.M. (2003) Executive coaching: an outcome study. *Consulting Psychology Journal: Practice and Research*, 55: 94–106.

Recommended books

De Haan, E. (2008) *Relational Coaching: Journeys Towards Mastering One-to-One Learning.* Chichester: John Wiley & Sons.

Palmer, S. and Whybrow, A. (2007) *Handbook of Coaching Psychology: A Guide for Practitioners.* London: Routledge.

Stober, D.R. and Grant, A.M. (2006) *Evidence Based Coaching Handbook: Putting Best Practices to Work for Your Clients.* Hoboken, NJ: Wiley.

3

Building on an interpersonal perspective on the coaching relationship

Alanna O'Broin and Stephen Palmer

Introduction

This chapter builds on the previous chapter's introduction of an interpersonal perspective on the coaching relationship. It spotlights through this conceptual lens of an interpersonal perspective five further topics particularly germane to the coaching relationship.

The first two topics, an exploration of the relevance and importance of the psychological contract in coaching, and a review of whether coaching relationships are improved with positive affect, are linked by the potential role of the coaching alliance or a component part of the coaching alliance in their effect. There are two links between the next three topics, on maximising the coachee's goal outcomes, coach–coachee matching, and the relevance of game theory to executive and business coaching. These links are the themes of relationship context and the increasing use of meta-cognitions and skills by the coach, within a complex coaching process. The chapter concludes by drawing together and summarising in bullet form its main points.

How relevant is the psychological contract in coaching?

A written contract

For most coaching assignments, the contracting process involves a written contract signed by both coach and coachee or if an organisational sponsor is present, by coach, coachee and organisational client (Bluckert, 2006). This written contract fulfils the functions of:

- establishing the objectives of the coaching;
- ensuring that both or all parties understand their responsibilities;
- clarifying the boundaries – of confidentiality, expectations of both or all parties, practical issues such as contact, availability and between-session assignments.

As Bachkirova (2007) notes, the alignment of the coachee's goals with those also useful to the organisation can define the timeframe and the involvement of different parties in evaluating outcomes of coaching assignments, as well as potentially creating ethical and confidentiality issues absent in other helping processes such as counselling.

The psychological contract and the coaching alliance

Whether or not a written contract is adopted, there exists within the coaching relationship a psychological 'contract' between coach and coachee. While early definitions of the psychological contract in the context of employment contracts emphasised *mutual expectations* of employee and organisation (Agyris, 1960; Levinson *et al.*, 1962), these mutual expectations, largely implicit and unspoken, were found to be difficult to operationalise and balance (Kotter, 1973). A later, more focused perspective implied that the psychological contract exists in the eye of each of the beholders (i.e. involving subjective beliefs) and concerns *mutual reciprocal obligations* rather than merely expectations:

> A major feature of psychological contracts is the individual's belief that the agreement is mutual, that is, a

common understanding exists that binds the parties involved to a particular course of action.

(Rousseau, 2001: 512)

Research on the psychological contract has focused more on the violation of, and disagreement in, the psychological contract, rather than its formation and revision, although researchers are turning to examination of how psychological contracts are formed (Shalk and Roe, 2007) in order to better identify those conditions in which *effective* psychological contracts can be created and revised. Rousseau (2001) identifies three concepts that are important in examining how psychological contracts are formed: schemas, promises and mutuality.

Schemas

Psychological contracts, as a form of schema, are expected to develop and emerge differently depending on whether sources of information are trusted, clear and explicit, and whether they are consistent.

Promises

Promises, whether verbal or from the interpretation of actions, are only meaningful as a promise when taken in context.

Mutuality

Mutuality requires both partners to hold the same beliefs regarding reciprocal obligations. Several necessary conditions in addition to perceived agreement need to exist for mutuality to occur:

- objective accuracy in individual perceptions;
- shared information between parties;
- the power or right to ask for terms considered to be in one's own interest;
- the right to consent or reject the terms of agreement.

Non-binding contracts, such as the psychological contract, are suggested 'to lead to personal attributions for co-operation and thus may provide an optimal basis for building interpersonal trust in a variety of situations' (Malhotra and Murnighan, 2002: 534).

Developing the theme of seeking to create and revise effective psychological contracts, this chapter suggests that the psychological contract can be conceptualised within the pantheoretic *coaching alliance*, in this case as described in the work of (Bordin, 1979, 1994) and in the later extension of Bordin's work (Hatcher and Barends, 2006). The psychological coaching contract conceptualised in this way can therefore act as a superordinate vehicle or container for purposive, collaborative coaching work, acting as a framework for its boundaries.

The concept of the alliance

Within the 'common factors' approach, the therapeutic alliance has been cited as the most consensual commonality across therapies (Greencavage and Norcross, 1990) and much research interest has been expended on establishing that the alliance is an important relationship factor linked to positive outcome (Norcross, 2002; Horvath, 2006), although a range of usages of the term 'alliance' also exists in the literature. Egan (2002) suggests that the *working alliance* (Bordin, 1979) can be used to bring together the best of the three approaches to the relationship (the relationship itself, the relationship as a means to an end, and the relationship and outcomes), and emphasises three aspects of this alliance:

- the collaborative nature of helping;
- the relationship as a forum for relearning;
- relationship flexibility.

In the work of Bordin (1979, 1994) and the later expansion of his work by Hatcher and Barends (2006), the term 'working alliance' is used to refer to the quality and strength of the collaborative relationship between client and therapist. Hatcher and Barends (2006) also suggest that the role of the client in negotiating the alliance was underplayed by Bordin. Emphasis on this definition of the alliance focuses on three primary features associated with purposive, collaborative work, those of *goals*, *tasks* and *bonds*.

The keyword in the coaching alliance, as in the psychological contract, is mutuality. In terms of:

- goals – there must be a clear mutual agreement about the goal of the work and the desired coaching outcome;
- tasks – there needs to be mutual understanding of how the coaching work will take place and the tasks or roles of each party;
- bonds – mutual empathy and respect need to exist.

In the process of explicitly discussing and agreeing the goals and tasks of the coaching it is posited that the conditions of clarity and transparency, which the coaching and coaching psychology literature confirm are a prerequisite to trust and respect, as well as ethical practice, are created. The mutual, collaborative process of agreeing the tasks and goals of coaching and reviewing these on an ongoing basis also acts as a helpful framework for the coach. In this way the coach's initial and ongoing assessment of the coachee's needs, values, personality, attitudes and context, and evaluation of their own suitability to meet the coachee's needs (see Bachkirova, 2007) can be monitored. It is important to note that this conceptualisation of the coaching alliance does not use alliance as a proxy for relationship, nor does it equate alliance with technique. Instead, the coaching alliance is an overarching stance from which to assess the degree, level and kind of collaborativeness and purposiveness of the coaching work that is required, and which is occurring.

Summary

This discussion has emphasised that the psychological 'contract' between coachee and coach is very important, both for ensuring clarity and transparency in the coaching process, and for providing a 'container' for the joint purposive work of coaching to take place. Conceptualising the psychological contract through the framework of the coaching alliance emphasises the collaborativeness, mutual influence and cooperation of coachee and coach, and the goal-focused nature of coaching in the coaching relationship. It also acts as a framework for the coach to monitor their ethical evaluation of their suitability for the coachee's needs, particularly in the event of a coachee's changing needs. The coaching alliance provides a vehicle for collaboration and co-creation and a space in which the coachee can feel safe and accepted enough to step into 'paradoxical bounded instability' where new forms of behaviour and creative action can happen (Cavanagh, 2006).

Are coaching relationships better with positive affect?

Humans as a species are physiologically influenced and regulated through their social relationships. Gilbert (2007) notes the recognition of multiple, complex processes that underlie our social behaviour and self-regulation, such as social motives to create positive affects in others about the self. By definition, this suggests that as coaches, some of what we are doing activates and deactivates key physiological systems in our coachees and *vice versa*.

Positive affect systems linked to social behaviour

A large literature exists on social support, illustrating the substantial physical and mental health benefits of befriending, particularly in times of stress (Taylor, 2007). One system of mental mechanisms involving *social safeness* of particular interest in this discussion is the social engagement system. This system inhibits activity in threat systems, deactivating fight/flight responses, as well as opening up alternative cognitive and emotional processing possibilities (Porges, 2001), and is linked to positive affect systems (Gilbert, 2007).

Recent research notes that there are at least two different types of positive affect systems, linked to different types of social behaviour. The *appetitive/seeking* aspects of motivation, related to dopaminergic systems, are linked to achievement seeking, control and avoidance of rejection and isolation, while the *contentment/soothing* aspects, related to oxytocin and opiate systems, are linked to affiliation, feelings of connectedness with others and calming effects (Depue and Morrone-Strupinsky, 2005). These and other researchers have suggested a neural basis for feeling safe, via a link between neuro-hormones such as oxytocin and affiliative behaviour (Carter, 1998; Wang, 2005). Emphasizing the role of oxytocin in stress regulation and social behaviour, the evolution of this link is suggested by the physiological need for attachment. These findings imply that feelings of safeness are stimulated by others rather than merely an absence of threat. In the coaching context this could suggest that the warmth that the coachee experiences from their coach in the coaching relationship could stimulate the contentment/soothing aspects of the positive affect system.

An optimal level of bond?

At this point it is useful to bring a discussion of the bond element of the coaching alliance back into play when considering positive affect. Bordin (1979) actually proposed two different bond concepts: one the broader *affective bond* involving liking, trust and respect, often referred to and emphasised by researchers (e.g. Martin *et al.*, 2000), as well as a second narrower bond concept, labelled the *work-supporting bond* by Hatcher and Barends (2006). With this second bond concept, the bond is seen as supportive to the goals and tasks, thus linking all three aspects to the core alliance issue – that of joint purposive work. This way of viewing the bond is useful in that an optimal level of bond for this particular coachee, within this particular conceptual framework, and in this particular context, can be sought. Indeed, too high a degree of liking and warmth may interfere with the coachee's disagreement about the tasks and goals of coaching, and feelings that the coach and coachee have towards each other may change (Bluckert, 2006). To paraphrase Hatcher and Barends (2006: 296), in the coaching context the question with this second bond concept is not: 'Do you like and respect your coach? but rather

'Do you like and respect your coach enough to do the work you expect to do in your coaching?'

Summary

So, is the coaching relationship better with positive affect? The evidence from neurophysiology suggests broadly yes, although further research is needed to clarify and explain more fully how these complex systems work and interact. Discussion of the bond element of the coaching alliance highlights the need for awareness of, and the ability to work with, the interpersonal dynamics of the particular relationship, with a particular coachee, in a particular conceptual framework and within a particular context. The aim of the coach is therefore to establish and maintain an optimal coaching alliance in which joint purposive work can be best achieved through the tasks and goals of coaching.

Maximising the coachee's goal outcomes

The coachee's ability and readiness to change is one of the seven major themes of the contextual model of coaching (Stober and Grant, 2006), while a collaborative working alliance is a second theme. The goal change literature (Sheldon and Kasser, 1995; Sheldon and Elliott, 1999; Sheldon *et al.*, 2003) suggests that greater goal attainment and satisfaction is associated with those goals aligned with the core personal interests and values of the coachee (Waring, 2008). Can the interpersonal interaction of the coach and coachee also help to maximise the coachee's goal outcomes? Interpersonal models and motivational theories on self-regulation will now be drawn upon to illustrate how this may be possible.

Self-regulation and partner responsiveness

Theories from social psychology on the interpersonal nature of the self have a long history (Cooley, 1902; Mead, 1934), with contemporary Interpersonal models emphasising the critical importance of close relationships to identification of self-hood (Baumeister, 1998) and the benefits of good relationships to emotional well-being (Hartup and Stevens, 1997). Motivational theories on self-regulating behaviour in close relationships (Sedikides and Strube, 1997; Carmichael *et al.*, 2007) describe the self as guiding decision-making and action as an active agent, through four self-regulatory motives:

- self-enhancement;
- self-verification;
- self-improvement;
- eliciting security and support from social relationships.

In close relationships, partners are seen as important sources of feedback in this self-regulation process, and perceiving their partners as *responsive* to their needs (Reis *et al.*, 2004; Reis, 2007) facilitates satisfaction of these motives.

Although the ripening relationship science field has historically focused primarily on (usually married) couples, existing evidence for the construct of *perceived partner responsiveness* suggests that these benefits extend to other types of relationships (Reis, 2007).

Self-regulation of the coachee

The coaching and coaching psychology literature has referred to the potential benefits of effective self-regulation from the viewpoint of the coach, citing the need for the coach's awareness of, and ability to manage, their own cognitive biases, such as attribution errors and confirmation bias (Kemp, 2008). Likewise, self-regulation is of benefit to the coachee (Grant, 2006), and may be impacted by the interpersonal processes of the coaching relationship.

Let us return to the self-regulatory motives outlined earlier, and take self-improvement as one example. The self-improvement motive is the desire to improve or advance one's attributes, skills and well-being (Sedikides and Strube, 1997) and close relationship partners often provide support and encouragement in the facilitation and achievement of their partner's goals and aspirations. In the coaching context, it is suggested that such encouragement of the coachee's movement towards intrinsic and self-determined extrinsic goals and values can be achieved in the form of *autonomy support* (Deci and Ryan, 1995; Mageau and Vallerand, 2003), which has been shown to be associated with positive outcomes in health care, learning and college students' close relationships. As previously noted (O'Broin and Palmer, 2007a), the autonomy-supportive style involves three factors that influence the coach's behaviours in the coaching relationship:

- the coach's orientation;
- the coaching context;
- the coach's perceptions of the coachee's behaviour and motivation.

There are suggestions that the autonomy-supportive style can be taught (Reeve, 1998).

Self-concordance

At the junction of the goal change a link has been postulated between self-concordance and coaching (Linley, 2004). Self-concordance is referred to by Grant (2007: 255) as 'the degree to which a goal is perceived by the individual as being autonomous'. Greater goal attainment and satisfaction are suggested to be associated with those self-concordant goals closely aligned with the core personal interests and values of the coachee (Waring, 2008). Burke and Linley (2007), in a preliminary study postulating that one mechanism of coaching effectiveness is through enhancing intrinsic motivation and enabling more self-concordant goals, found that senior managers in business demonstrated a significant increase in goal self-concordance and commitment to the goal following a single one-to-one coaching session.

Summary

Burke and Linley's (2007) study demonstrated that raising a coachee's levels of self-concordance with their goals is one mechanism through which coaching may effectively support goal attainment support (see also Grant, 2006: 162 for a discussion of self-concordant goals). Drawing upon the relationship science studies cited above, which point to the facility for close relationships to provide the conducive context for the effective fulfilment of self-regulatory motives, can develop the discussion further. A role for inter-personal interaction and mutual influence in the coaching relationship is postulated to help achieve such self-concordance and autonomy of the coachee, as described in the discussion above.

The finding in the relationship science literature of partner responsiveness as an important source of feedback in the self-regulation process, and highlighted in the coach-ing context with the finding that coach qualities such as responsiveness are linked to better outcomes (de Haan, 2008; de Haan *et al.*, 2008), could suggest a role for appropriate responsiveness in an iterative, sequential process (as previ-ously discussed by O'Broin and Palmer, 2007a). These examples are just two of a number of possible ways in which self-regulation motives may benefit from interpersonal interaction and mutual influencing in the coaching relation-ship, which further discussion and research in this area could reveal.

Coach–coachee matching

Matching of coach and coachee in the broad sense of the terms has been conducted in coaching in relation to a num-ber of factors in organisational, technical and interpersonal contexts (Law *et al.*, 2007: 205). However, coach–coachee matching of single, surface-level diversity factors, of gender (Sparrow, 2006), culture and age, as well as deeper diversity factors, such as personality (Scoular and Linley, 2006), has limited representation in the coaching research literature, with mixed results (Wycherley and Cox, 2008). 'Cognitive similarity' is a factor noted to have enhanced the coaching relationship, in aiding the formation and maintenance of rapport in the therapeutic relationship (Hunt *et al.*, 1985), and improved sustainability of year-long relationships between mentor and mentees on a 'virtual' mentoring pro-gramme in higher education (Beddoes-Jones and Miller, 2006). With regard to the broader concept of 'modality similarity', Herman (1998) found that similarity in therapist–client pairings on the Structural Profile Inventory from multimodal therapy (Lazarus, 1989, 1993) had a positive impact on psychotherapy outcome, possibly through enhancement of rapport and enabling clearer communication and with techniques being delivered more 'on target'. This finding suggests the potentially advantageous use of the multimodal approach in coaching (Richards, 1999; Palmer *et al.*, 2003; Palmer and Gyllensten, 2008).

Individual identity as the entry point to the coachee's culture

Remaining on the topic of coach–coachee matching, and taking culture as our focus, we can appreciate that culture is an important influence in all coaching relationships (Rosinksi and Abbott, 2006). By the same token, unhelpful or negative stereotyping, or generalising about culture, requires caution (Law, 2008). Taking individual identity as the entry point to culture, the intercultural coaching approach (Rosinski, 2003) brings together research on cultural differences into a cultural orientations framework (COF), which summarises orientations across which people differ, including definitions of identity and purpose, organisational arrangements, communication patterns, sense of power and responsibility, time management approaches, and notions of territory and boundaries. Intercultural coaching is pragmatic, drawing upon ideas that work in the coachee's context, with measures of success determined by the coachee.

Summary

The context model of selection and matching in executive coaching (Wycherley and Cox, 2008) is pertinent to this discussion in emphasising the complex interpersonal and systemic nature of the matching process, as well as highlighting the dangers in attempting to match coachee and coach on single, surface-level diversity factors. These authors also suggest the benefit of helping executive coachees learn how best to use the coaching process and that the coach's experience is an important consideration in the selection process.

This particular 'individual identity' aspect of matching has been emphasised to illustrate the point that the concept of matching may be more relevant when viewed in the sense of the coach matching their stance, experience and interventions to the specific needs of the coachee in their specific context (Lazarus, 1993). Thus 'matching' becomes more a case of 'tailoring' the relationship at a finer degree of specification than 'matching' on a situational diversity variable such as age or gender or a multiple of such variables, at a higher level of generalisation.

Game theory's relevance to executive and business coaching

As was outlined in the previous chapter, relationship science researchers now concur that *interactions* between the partners of a relationship are its essence, and that *mutual influence* is the hallmark of such interactions (Kelley *et al.*, 1983; Berscheid and Reis, 1998; Reis, 2007). The co-created coaching relationship is therefore shaped by the unfolding interactional sequence of its participants' communications, and the coach and coachee's biases and schemas may influence positively or deleteriously this co-construction process. As has previously been suggested, a game theory analogy (O'Broin and Palmer, 2007a: 301; 2007b) can be used to model this interactional sequence in the coaching relationship. Two-person 'games', such as in the coaching dyad, can be *competitive* or *cooperative*, the latter involving coordinated strategies in order to achieve the best outcome for both parties.

Reciprocal causation

Leahy (2007), in applying a game metaphor to the therapeutic relationship, highlights that games involve *reciprocal causation*, the evaluation of feedback and iterative moves made by the other participant in the 'game'. Reciprocal causation could be considered akin to *appropriate responsiveness* in the coaching relationship context (O'Broin and Palmer, 2007a: 312; see also Newman *et al.*, 2006). As the coach and coachee follow their own internal rules as these sequences unfold, self-fulfilling prophecies about the beliefs and opinions of the coach and coachee may occur.

Attribution errors and cognitive biases

Recent discussion in the coaching psychology literature illustrates this latter point. Citing Heider (1958) and attribution theory, Kemp (2008) discusses the *fundamental attribution error* (Ross, 1977) where the tendency is for the observer to overestimate the dispositional factors of individuals' behaviour and underestimate the situational factors of a given situation. Kemp (2008) argues the salience of this error in coaching within organisational or corporate settings, with the complex nature of team and group working, where a coachee may attribute their poor performance to the incompetence of others or market conditions. *Behavioural confirmation* (Snyder, 1984), where people tend to behave over time as people expect them to, partly as a result of the observer's influence on the behaviour of the observed, is a further bias identified as pertinent to coaching. Finally, and in Kemp's view perhaps one of the most debilitating cognitive biases, is the *overconfidence bias* (Gilovich *et al.*, 2002) – the tendency of the coaching psychologist to overestimate the accuracy of their opinions and beliefs and be overconfident in them. All these biases can diminish the ability of the coach to be objective in the coaching relationship. Kemp (2008) suggests the importance for the coaching psychologist of self-management, in which the coach develops deeper self-awareness of their cognitive, behavioural, perceptual and emotional systems, as well as developing self-insight and adaptive capability, to enable effective management of the coach's influence and impact of their unique psychological system on that of their coachee.

Summary

As we have seen, applying a game analogy to the coaching relationship can be instructive in spotlighting how some coachees could approach coaching (O'Broin and Palmer, 2007b), how coach and coachee biases can influence the interpersonal process of the coaching dialogue, and how the coach can, through a process of professional development, improve their self-awareness and self-management in the service of their individual coachee's needs in the unique dynamic of each coaching relationship.

Conclusions

This chapter has further explored and developed an interpersonal perspective on the coaching relationship by addressing five topics relevant to this discussion. The main conclusions reached in this discussion are provided below in bullet point form:

- The psychological contract is important as a framework for joint ongoing evaluation of the coachee-led needs of the coaching, as well as the coach's ethical and experience-led assessment of their abilities and responses in meeting those needs.
- The psychological contract of coaching may operate via the coaching alliance as a vehicle for the joint purposive work of the coaching, through its goals, tasks and bonds.
- Feelings of safeness may be actively stimulated by the coach, perhaps through the coachee's experience of warmth from their coach.
- The *work-supportive bond* – an optimal level of bond supportive to the goals and tasks of coaching – may be preferable to a broader affective bond.
- Constructive interpersonal interaction and mutual influence in the coaching relationship may contribute to the achievement of self-concordance and autonomy to help maximise the coachee's goal outcomes.
- Matching coach and coachee is a complex interpersonal and systemic process in which surface-level diversity factors are unlikely to prove effective and in which the coach's experience is likely to be an important consideration.
- Using an 'individual identity' approach, matching may

be more appropriate if conceptualised as 'tailoring' the coaching at a finer degree of specification to the coachee's needs, personality and context, than matching on a surface-level diversity factor at a higher level of generalisation.

- Applying a game theory analogy highlights how coach and coachee biases can influence positively or detrimentally the interpersonal dialogue and processes in the coaching relationship.
- By improving self-awareness at a meta level, coaches can improve their self-management in the service of their coachee's needs.

Reflective questions

- Do you think that game theory is important in the coach–coachee and mentor–mentee relationship?
- Does matching the coach and coachee really impact upon coaching outcomes?
- Is the coach–coachee relationship comparable with the therapist–client relationship?
- How important is the unwritten psychological contract?

References

Agyris, C. (1960) *Understanding Organizational Behavior*. London: Tavistock Publications.

Bachkirova, T. (2007) Role of coaching psychology in defining boundaries between counselling and coaching. In S. Palmer and A. Whybrow (eds) *Handbook of Coaching Psychology: A Guide for Practitioners*. London: Routledge.

Baumeister, R.F. (1998) The self. In D.T. Gilbert, S.T. Fiske and G. Lindzey (eds) *The Handbook of Social Psychology* (4th ed., pp. 680–740). New York: McGraw-Hill.

Beddoes-Jones, F. and Miller, J. (2006) 'Virtual' mentoring: can the principle of cognitive pairing increase its effectiveness? *International Journal of Evidence Based Coaching and Mentoring*, 4: 54–60.

Berscheid, E. and Reis, H.T. (1998) Attraction and close relationships. In D.T. Gilbert, S.T. Fiske and G. Lindzey (eds) *The*

Handbook of Social Psychology (4th ed., vol. 2, pp. 193–281). New York: McGraw-Hill.

Bluckert, P. (2006) *Psychological Dimensions of Executive Coaching*. Maidenhead: McGraw-Hill.

Bordin, E.S. (1979) The generalisability of the psychoanalytic concept of the working alliance. *Psychotherapy: Theory, Research and Practice*, 16: 252–260.

Bordin, E.S. (1994) Theory and research on the therapeutic working alliance: new directions. In A.O. Horvath and L.S. Greenberg (eds) *The Working Alliance: Theory, Research and Practice*. New York: Wiley.

Burke, D. and Linley, P.A. (2007) Enhancing goal self-concordance through coaching. *International Coaching Psychology Review*, 2: 62–69.

Carmichael, C.L., Fen-Fang, T., Smith, S.M., Caprariello, P.A. and Reis, H.T. (2007) Self and intimate relationships. In C. Sedikides and S.J. Spencer (eds) *The Self*. New York: Psychology Press.

Carter, C.S. (1998) Neuroendocrine perspectives on social attachment and love. *Psychoneuroendocrinology*, 23: 779–818.

Cavanagh, M. (2006) Coaching from a systemic perspective: a complex adaptive conversation. In D.R. Stober and A.M. Grant (eds) *Evidence Based Coaching Handbook: Putting Best Practices to Work for Your Clients*. Hoboken, NJ: John Wiley & Sons.

Cooley, C.H. (1902) *Human Nature and the Social Order*. New York: Scribner.

de Haan, E. (2008) *Relational Coaching: Journeys Towards Mastering One-to-One Learning*. Chichester: John Wiley & Sons.

de Haan, E., Culpin, V. and Curd, J. (2008) Executive coaching in practice: what determines helpfulness for coachees? *Consulting Psychology Journal: Practice and Research*, submitted.

Deci, E.L. and Ryan, R.M. (1995) Human autonomy: the basis for true self-esteem. In M.H. Kernis (ed.) *Efficacy, Agency and Self-Esteem* (pp. 31–49). New York: Plenum Press.

Depue, R.A. and Morrone-Strupinsky, J.V. (2005) A neurobehavioral model of affiliative bonding. *Behavioral and Cognitive Neuroscience Reviews*, 28: 313–395.

Egan, G. (2002) *The Skilled Helper: A Problem-Management and Opportunity-Development Approach to Helping* (7th ed.). Pacific Grove, CA: Brooks/Cole.

Gilbert, P. (2007) Evolved minds and compassion in the therapeutic relationship. In P. Gilbert and R.L. Leary (eds) *The Therapeutic Relationship in the Cognitive Behavioral Psychotherapies*. London: Routledge.

Gilovich, T., Griffin, D. and Kahnemann, E. (eds) (2002) *Heuristics and Biases: The Psychology of Intuitive Judgement*. Cambridge: Cambridge University Press.

Grant, A.M. (2006) An integrative goal-focused approach to executive coaching. In D.R. Stober and A.M. Grant (eds) *Evidence-Based Coaching Handbook: Putting Best Practices to Work for Your Clients*. Hoboken, NJ: John Wiley.

Grant, A.M. (2007) A model of goal striving and mental health for coaching populations. *International Coaching Psychology Review*, 2: 248–262.

Greencavage, L.M. and Norcross, J.C. (1990) Where are the commonalities among the therapeutic common factors? *Professional Psychology: Research and Practice*, 21: 372–378.

Hartup, W.W. and Stevens, N. (1997) Friendships and adaptation in the life course. *Psychological Bulletin*, 121: 355–370.

Hatcher, R.L. and Barends, A.W. (2006) How a return to theory could help alliance research. *Psychotherapy: Theory, Research, Practice, Training*, 43: 292–299.

Heider, F. (1958) *The Psychology of Interpersonal Relations*. New York: Wiley.

Herman, S.M. (1998) The relationship between therapist–client modality similarity and psychotherapy outcome. *Journal of Psychotherapy Practice and Research*, 7: 56–64.

Horvath, A.O. (2006) The alliance in context: accomplishments, challenges and future directions. *Psychotherapy: Theory, Research, Practice, Training*, 43: 258–263.

Hunt, D.D., Carr, J.E., Dagodakis, C.S. and Walker, E.A. (1985) Cognitive match as a predictor of psychotherapy outcome. *Psychotherapy*, 22: 718–721.

Kelley, H.H., Berscheid, E., Christensen, A., Harvey, J.H., Huston, T.L., Levinger, G., McClintock, E., Peplau, L.A. and Peterson, D.R. (1983) *Close Relationships*. New York: Freeman.

Kemp, T. (2008) Self management and the coaching relationship. *International Coaching Psychology Review*, 3: 32–42.

Kotter, J.P. (1973) The psychological contract. *California Management Review*, 15: 91–99.

Law, H. (2008) Diversity coaching. *People and Organisations @ Work*: 6–7.

Law, H.L., Ireland, S. and Hussain, Z. (2007) Conclusion, discussion and future work. In H. Law, S. Ireland and Z. Hussain *The Psychology of Coaching, Mentoring and Learning*. Chichester: John Wiley.

Lazarus, A.A. (1989) *The Practice of Multimodal Therapy*. Balimore, MD: John Hopkins University Press.

Lazarus, A.A. (1993) Tailoring the therapeutic relationship or being an authentic chameleon. *Psychotherapy*, 3: 404–407.

Leahy, R.L. (2007) Schematic mismatch in the therapeutic relationship: a social-cognitive model. In P. Gilbert and R.L. Leary (eds) *The Therapeutic Relationship in the Cognitive Behavioral Psychotherapies*. London: Routledge.

Levinson, H., Price, C.R., Munden, K.J., Mandl, H.J. and Solley, C.M. (1962) *Men, Management and Mental Health*. Cambridge, MA: Harvard University Press.

Linley, P.A. (2004) Business and executive coaching: a positive psychology perspective. Paper presented at the Meyer Campbell Business Coach Alumni Seminar, London.

Mageau, G.A. and Vallerand, R.J. (2003) The coach–athlete relationship: a motivational model. *Journal of Sports Sciences*, 21: 883–904.

Malhotra, D. and Murnighan, J.K. (2002) The effects of contracts on interpersonal trust. *Administrative Science Quarterly*, 47: 534–559.

Martin, D.J., Garske, J.P. and Davis, M.K. (2000) Relation of the therapeutic alliance with outcome and other variables: a meta-analytic review. *Journal of Consulting and Clinical Psychology*, 68: 438–450.

Mead, G.H. (1934) *Mind, Self and Society*. Chicago, IL: University of Chicago Press.

Newman, M.G., Stiles, W.B., Janeck, A. and Woody, S.R. (2006) Integration of therapeutic factors in anxiety disorders. In L.G. Castonguay and L.E. Beutler (eds) *Principles of Therapeutic Change that Work*. Oxford: Oxford University Press.

Norcross, J.C. (2002) *Psychotherapy Relationships that Work*. Oxford: Oxford University Press.

O'Broin, A. and Palmer, S. (2007a) Reappraising the coach–client relationship: the unassuming change agent in coaching. In S. Palmer and A. Whybrow (eds) *Handbook of Coaching Psychology: A Guide for Practitioners*. London: Routledge.

O'Broin, A. and Palmer, S. (2007b) Expanding horizons in understanding the coach–client relationship. Symposium paper presented at the 3rd Annual National Coaching Psychology Conference, British Psychological Society, London, 17 December.

Palmer, S. and Gyllensten, K. (2008) How cognitive behavioural, rational emotive behavoural or multimodal coaching could prevent mental health problems, enhance performance and reduce work related stress. *Journal of Rational-Emotive Cognitive-Behavioural Therapy*, 26: 38–52.

Palmer, S., Cooper, C. and Thomas, K. (2003) *Creating a Balance: Managing Stress*. London: British Library.

Porges, S.W. (2001) The polyvagal theory: phylogenetic substrates of a social nervous system. *International Journal of Psychophysiology*, 42: 123–146.

Reeve, J. (1998) Autonomy support as an interpersonal motivating style: is it teachable? *Contemporary Educational Psychology*, 23: 312–330.

Reis, H.T. (2007) Steps towards the ripening of relationship science. *Personal Relationships*, 14: 1–23.

Reis, H.T., Clark, M.S. and Holmes, J.G. (2004) Perceived partners responsiveness as an organizing construct in the study of intimacy and closeness. In D. Mashek and A. Aron (eds) *The Handbook of Closeness and Intimacy* (pp. 201–225). Mahwah, NJ: Lawrence Erlbaum Associates.

Richards, J.T. (1999) Multimodal therapy: a useful model for the executive coach. *Consulting Psychology Journal: Practice and Research*, 51: 24–30.

Rosinski, P. (2003) *Coaching across Cultures: New Tools for Leveraging National, Corporate and Professional Differences*. London: Nicholas Brearley.

Rosinski, P. and Abbott, G. (2006) Intercultural coaching. In J. Passmore (ed.) *Excellence in Coaching: The Industry Guide*. London: Kogan Page.

Ross, L. (1977) The intuitive psychologist and his shortcomings: distortions in the attribution process. In L. Berkowitz (ed.) *Advances in Experimental Social Psychology* (vol. 10, pp. 173–240). Orlando, FL: Academic Press.

Rousseau, D.M. (2001) Schema, promise and mutuality: the building blocks of the psychological contract. *Journal of Occupational and Organizational Psychology*, 74: 511–541.

Schalk, R. and Roe, R.E. (2007) Towards a dynamic model of the psychological contract. *Journal for the Theory of Social Behaviour*, 37: 167–181.

Scoular, A. and Linley, P.A. (2006) Coaching, goal-setting and personality type: what matters? *The Coaching Psychologist*, 2: 9–11.

Sedikides, C. and Struber, M.J. (1997) Self-evaluation: to thine own self be good, to thine own self be sure, to thine own self be true, and to thine own self be better. In M.P. Zanna (ed.) *Advances in Experimental Social Psychology* (pp. 209–269). New York: Academic Press.

Sheldon, K.M. and Elliot, A.J. (1999) Goal striving, need satisfaction, and longitudinal well-being: the Self-Concordance Model. *Journal of Personality and Social Psychology*, 76: 482–497.

Sheldon, K.M. and Kasser, T. (1995) Coherence and congruence: two aspects of personality integration. *Journal of Personality and Social Psychology*, 68: 531–543.

Sheldon, K.M., Arndt, J. and Houser-Marko, L. (2003) In search of the organismic valuing process: the human tendency to move towards beneficial goal choices. *Journal of Personality*, 71: 835–869.

Snyder, M. (1984) When belief creates reality. In L. Berkowitz (ed.) *Advances in Experimental Social Psychology* (vol. 18, pp. 116, 167). New York: Academic Press.

Sparrow, S. (2006) The gender gap. *Training and Coaching Today*, April: 22–23.

Stober, D.R. and Grant, A.M. (2006) Toward a contextual approach to coaching models. In D.R. Stober and A.M. Grant (eds) *Evidence Based Coaching Handbook: Putting Best Practices to Work for Your Clients*. Hoboken, NJ: Wiley.

Taylor, S.E. (2007) Social support. In H.S. Friedman and R.C. Silver (eds) *Foundations of Health Psychology* (pp. 145–171). New York: Oxford University Press.

Wang, S. (2005) A conceptual framework for integrating research related to the physiology of compassion and the wisdom of Buddhist teachings. In P. Gilbert (ed.) *Compassion: Conceptualisations, Research and Use in Psychotherapy* (pp. 75–120). London: Routledge.

Waring, P.A. (2008) Coaching the brain. *The Coaching Psychologist*, 4: 63–70.

Wycherley, I.M. and Cox, E. (2008) Factors in the selection and matching of executive coaches in organizations. *Coaching: An International Journal of Theory, Research and Practice*, 1: 39–53.

Recommended books

Castonguay, L.G. and Beutler, L.E. (eds) (2006) *Principles of Therapeutic Change that Work*. Oxford: Oxford University Press.

De Haan, E. (2008) *Relational Coaching: Journeys Towards Mastering One-to-One Learning*. Chichester: John Wiley & Sons.

Norcross, J.C. (2002) *Psychotherapy Relationships that Work*. Oxford: Oxford University Press.

Palmer, S. and Whybrow, A. (2007) *Handbook of Coaching Psychology: A Guide for Practitioners*. London: Routledge.

4

Feeding back, feeding forward and setting goals

Almuth McDowall and Lynne Millward

Magic Mirror on the Wall, who is the Fairest one of all?
(Popular quote from *Snow White* by the Brothers Grimm)

Introduction

Feedback is everywhere in life – we get it from people, the tasks that we do, and in fairytales even from a magic mirror. But to what extent do we understand the impact of feedback on relationships? Consider the question above, asked by the Queen in the tale *Snow White* to ascertain whether she is the most beautiful woman in her kingdom. What the Queen wants to hear from the magic mirror is the reply 'Thou, O Queen, art the fairest of all'. However, as the young Snow White grows into a rival beauty, the magic mirror changes its answer to an honest 'O Lady Queen, though fair ye be, Snow-White is fairer far to see'. Some of us may remember the impact of this feedback, as the Queen subsequently tries to assassinate Snow White in a number of ways. We can surmise that a number of emotions are responsible for this rather drastic reaction, such as anger, disappointment and jealousy. While the Queen took to drastic measures that we are unlikely to encounter in the real world in coaching, the example nevertheless illustrates the potential consequences of negative and unexpected feedback. In many ways, feedback is about holding up a mirror and saying 'this is what you do/what you are like in the eyes of others'. A skilful coach may achieve this through the processing of existing information, questioning, challenging, set tasks and the evaluation of any processes, as well as conveying factual knowledge and other information. However, these basic processes need to be *effective* in the context of the coaching relationship to result in desired outcomes.

Therefore, this chapter will elucidate feedback in terms of both process and content, with a particular focus on both the role of interpersonal relationships and potential outcomes, such as performance and mood. We use case studies and real-life examples to illustrate how feedback effects need to be understood in the dynamic context of coaching. We argue that feeding back information on the effectiveness of past behaviours is by itself unlikely to harness coachees with sufficient impetus for positive change. Feedback needs to be combined with mutually negotiated goals in the here and now, and a vision for the future to activate and sustain motivation. We draw from diverse theoretical interventions such as Feedback Intervention Theory (FIT; Kluger and DeNisi, 1996), Theory of Possible Selves (Markus and Nurius, 1986), Goal Setting (e.g. Locke and Latham, 1990), theories of motivation such as Control Theory (Carver and Scheier, 1981) and Regulatory Focus Theory (Higgins, 1997) as well as Appreciative Enquiry (e.g. Cooperrider and Srivastava, 1987). While our primary focus is on coaching and relationships in the context of work, we broaden our argument to include research from the educational and other applied domains to ensure that this chapter is applicable to coaches in a variety of settings. We conclude with suggestions for improving coaching practice and further reading.

Introduction to feedback

In essence, feedback is information about a process or behaviour that is relayed from one party to another (see McDowall, 2008, for a full introductory review). In the context of coaching, this content usually pertains to behaviours or levels of performance on the part of the coachee. Examples are summarised in Table 4.1. We note that in addition to feedback on *content* there is also *process feedback*, for instance when there are blocks to progression on the part of the coachee (or coach, for that matter) or impasses/plateaus.

Table 4.1 Examples of feedback in coaching

Feedback source	Examples of content feedback	Examples of process feedback	Feedback recipient
The coach	Feedback on the topics that coachees bring to the session	Feedback on the coachee's progress, such as how the coachee took to 'homework' in-between sessions. Also feedback on real-time exercises or role plays during the coaching session	The coachee
Psychometric profile, relayed by the coach	Discussion of the actual profile, such as personality preferences	Discussion of how the coachee makes sense of the profile – to what extent does it ring true?	The coachee
360-degree feedback profile, either commissioned by the coach or from pre-existing data	Structured feedback on the actual ratings on a number of scales, with particular reference to potential differences in comparison to the self-evaluation	Making explicit and acknowledging how the coachee reacts, and what this is saying about the feedback process	The coachee
The coachee	Reactions to the content of the coaching sessions – are these appropriate, pitched at the right level?	Reactions to the coaching process: are there particularly functional or dysfunctional aspects of the relationship?	The coach, potentially also the commissioning client

(*Continued overleaf*)

Table 4.1 Continued

Feedback source	Examples of content feedback	Examples of process feedback	Feedback recipient
The task	Is the content (requirements, obligations, expectations) of the current job/role/task aligned with capabilities? What evidence is there that can be used to look closely at performance (e.g. appraisal documents, performance outcomes)?	Specific aspects of the task that may evoke reactions such as boredom, stimulation and frustration on the one hand or joy, happiness and fulfilment on the other	The coach and/or coachee

Most of the examples provided in Table 4.1 relate to structured and pre-planned feedback, such as the discussion of a psychometric profile. Feedback can also happen unprompted and/or informally, such as through ongoing feedback on the coachee's progress over a number of coaching sessions. Note that our examples primarily refer to a 'top-down' process where the coach provides feedback to the coachee, as feedback may happen less frequently the other way round, particularly in specific activities such as executive coaching where there might be a mandate to 'achieve' and move the coach along swiftly. (This has implications for the coaching relationship, in terms of power dynamics and perceived authority and credibility, and we return to this point later in this chapter.) There is clearly a need for process feedback to be legitimate in the coaching relationship from coachee to coach. Coachees should have the mandate to put forward requests such as:

- I need you to be firmer with me about [a particular issue or range of issues].

- I like it when you/don't like it so much when you [do something, say something].
- I need more structure from you/less structure from you to help me [achieve something].
- When you do [example] this makes me feel [particular emotion]. Could you be more/less [example]?

According to Feedback Intervention Therapy [FIT] (Kluger and DeNisi, 1996), feedback also originates from the task itself, as for instance tasks that are perceived as boring or frustrating might elicit reactions of resentment or even anger. For example, all of us can relate to what we perceive to be unnecessary paperwork, which can be avoided to some extent but which lands on you like an elephant on a mouse if you don't get it done when you should. The feedback is negative, as the task is burdensome and this results in apprehension and reluctance to get things done. Task feedback can of course be positive, where this is stimulating or rewarding. For example, teachers or instructors can be vicariously rewarded via the success of their students.

In a coaching context, feedback reactions to the task can of course come from both the coach and coachee. This might have particular implications for the relationship where these are different from each other. For example, the coach could experience frustration that the coachee is not progressing in the anticipated way while the coachee is quite happy with progress. Or *vice versa*, the coachee might feel frustrated with a lack of progress, whereas the coach thinks that progress is all fine. We present an example in Text Box 4.1.

Text Box 4.1   Dealing with different perceptions in a coaching relationship

Sam, the coachee, has been having coaching by Parvinder, the coach, over a number of sessions. The initial goal for the sessions was to help Sam overcome her fear of giving presentations to clients. Parvinder is pleased that Sam is doing homework in-between sessions (such as reading up on presentation skills, working through practical exercises as well as practising relaxation skills) and is in her view progressing well. Parvinder communicates her satisfaction with the process to Sam. This results in an unexpected outburst. Sam is voicing frustration, as in the coachee's view the homework is too repetitive and lacks the link to improving presentation skills in real-life settings as much as initially hoped.

Reflective questions

- What could be the reasons for the differences in perception?
- How could Sam and Parvinder use feedback effectively to move the coaching sessions forward?
- In what way could you differentiate between process and content feedback, and use either or both to maximum effect?

Having outlined some of the basic issues with regards to feedback in coaching, we will now turn to how these are supported by the research literature.

Feeding back: theory and implications

The extant body of evidence on feedback effects is mixed, and has little to say about the differences between process and content. The fundamental assumption is that feedback will impact on human performance, and thus change behaviour in some way (see McDowall, 2008, for a full review). The seminal meta-analysis by Kluger and DeNisi (1996) that combined data from various areas of psychology showed, however, that performance improvements following feedback were overall relatively modest, and in fact performance deteriorated for a third of the total observations included. The authors proposed FIT to guide future research, which considers a complex number of factors such as the origin of the feed-back, characteristics of the feedback message and also the recipient. However, this theory cannot explain why posi-tive feedback sometimes motivates others and sometimes it does not; likewise negative feedback can have a motivat-ing or de-motivating effect. In the context of performance feedback at work, the link between feedback and perform-ance is also modest (Smither *et al.*, 2005). However, behaviour changes are more likely to take place if feedback is sup-ported by executive coaching following feedback sessions compared with feedback that is not paired with coaching, because the latter facilitates effective goal setting (Smither *et al.*, 2003).

The implications of the research evidence are two-fold. First, that the direct link between feedback and performance improvements remains small. However, this increases if individuals are encouraged to set more concrete and future-directed goals with a coach. The lack of follow-through in feedback activities has been lamented as the 'Achilles' heel' (London *et al.*, 1997), which provides a rationale for the one-to-one support from coaching in organisational contexts.

Several observations might account for this. First, per-formance itself is feedback as we outlined earlier that feedback does not have to come from people. Individual per-formance, or rather specific indicators thereof, provides a benchmark of where individuals are in relation to others or in relation to their own goals. Such performance feedback might be relayed in different ways and it also matters how aware the recipients of the feedback are. Feedback is in essence a process of relaying information from one party to another: the 'sender' conveys a 'message' to a 'recipient' (see McDowall, 2008). Going back to our earlier example, this process is akin to holding up a mirror in front of someone else. However, it matters how the mirror is held and whether people can recognise their reflection. If people can't see themselves clearly, feedback is unlikely to have any effect. Two different explanations could account for this. People might be 'blind' to their reflection (so unaware of what they are like in others' eyes) or alternatively the lack of a mirror image might be due to the fact that the mirror is not positioned appropriately, so that people find it difficult to see themselves. We illustrate this with two examples from a coaching context in Text Box 4.2.

The examples in Text Box 4.2 show that even seemingly simple feedback processes can be complex. There is not one

---

Text Box 4.2   Using the 'feedback mirror'

Scenario 1

Coach A is explaining a 360-degree feedback profile to coachee B (where performance ratings from different sources are compared to a self-rating), which indicates that B might need to concentrate on optimising interpersonal communication. B is unreceptive to the idea, as 'my team is just not bright enough to understand my ideas'.

Scenario 2

Coach C and coachee D are going through a psychometric profile, which provides information about D's personal preferences and areas of competence in the workplace scale by scale. D is getting short-tempered and frustrated and ready to walk out of the session, saying 'I can't take all of this in – and it isn't like me anyway!'

Reflective questions

- What are the differences and commonalities between Scenario 1 and Scenario 2?
- To what extent should the 'feedback mirror' be repositioned?
- How can coaches facilitate self-awareness (seeing myself in the same way that other people do)?

feedback theory that considers the interactivity of relationships in sufficient depth. Feedback is a dynamic process rather than a discrete event, and we argue that it is this fluidity, combined with the fact that we all subtly differ in our expectations and approaches to feedback, that has made the theoretical links between feedback and performance elusive to date. At a minimum, a comprehensive feedback theory should cover:

• individual differences;
• consideration of the process;
• consideration of content;
• how goals are addressed;
• the importance of relationships.

We summarise several relevant theories in Table 4.2, to guide our readers and offer suggestions for further reading.

As can be seen, very few theories actively consider the process and the role of relationships. Another issue that needs to be highlighted here is the crucial role of the self. FIT (Kluger and DeNisi, 1996) proposes that feedback is more likely to be detrimental if it is directed towards the self, rather than towards the task. Other theories challenge the notion that the self is a unitary construct. Regulatory Focus Theory (Higgins, 1997) holds that there are three aspects of the self: the actual, ideal and ought self. Behaviour may be directed to address potential discrepancies between people's actual and ideal self, or to discrepancies between actual and ought self. These 'self variables' are associated with two different motivational states: (a) promotion focus or approval and (b) prevention focus or avoidance. The tension between these motivational states in a coaching context is illustrated in Text Box 4.3.

From a coaching point of view, it is also useful to locate goal setting in the context of past, present and future selves. Future selves have been termed 'possible selves' and pertain to representations of self-in-the-future, which are essentially cognitions that guide our behaviour, which in turn partially determines what we actually become in the future (Markus and Nurius, 1986; Markus and Ruvolo, 1989). Most pertinently from a coaching point of view is that possible selves

Table 4.2 Overview of theories and frameworks relevant to feedback

Theory	Does this theory consider individual differences of the feedback source?	Does this theory consider individual differences of the feedback recipient?	Does this theory consider feedback content?	Does this theory consider feedback processes?	Does this theory consider goals?	Does this theory consider the impact of feedback on relationships?	Seminal reference
Feedback Intervention Theory	✓	✓	✓	Implicitly yes	✗	✗	Kluger and DeNisi (1996)
Regulatory Focus Theory	✓	✗	✓		✓	✗	Higgins (1997)
Theory of Possible Selves	✓	✗	✓	✗	✗	✗	Markus and Nurius (1986); Markus and Ruvolo (1989)
Psychometric Perspective – Focus on Predictive Validity	✓	✗	✓	✗	✓ (not all studies)	✗	For example Smither et al. (2005)

	Judge et al. (1997)	Locke and Latham (1990)	Cooperrider and Srivastava (1987)	Seligman (2000)
Core Self-Evaluations	✓	✓	✗	✗
Goal Setting	✓	✓	✗	✗
Appreciative Enquiry	✗	✗	✓	✓
Positive Psychology	✗	✗	✓	✓

Text Box 4.3   Example for understanding ideal and actual selves

Katy is a human resources (HR) manager who seeks the approval of others to validate her 'ideal self' as perfect and mostly fulfils this self-expectation. However, when she makes mistakes or is at the receiving end of criticism, Katy finds it hard to reconcile her self-expectations with her experienced reality. She responds by putting even more pressure on herself and admonishing herself for her apparent imperfection, sometimes becoming overwhelmingly anxious and emotionally disabled by feelings of failure. At the same time, she finds herself avoiding situations in which she might – in her own mind – become exposed as 'less than perfect'. Situations that she finds herself avoiding are in particular those in which she has less control over her performance and thus less control over how she is evaluated by others whose opinions matter to her. In her job, these situations arise when she relies on rapport building as the means of securing particular HR outcomes in a working environment in which there is resistance to being 'policed by HR'. A recent restructuring at work has meant reapplying for jobs that have all been radically reworked and put under new terms and conditions. Although she has been encouraged to apply for a new job for which she is deemed by her line manager as being especially well suited, and on one level, also she perceives that she 'could do the job' (it would also mean promotion and a salary increase), she is held back by self-doubts from applying. She seeks the help of a coaching psychologist to help her negotiate the options she has – give her notice in, take the redundancy money and become self-employed, apply for the new more challenging reframed job, or apply for a lower-key job more consistent with her 'current job'. The last of these options will mean that she can stay in her comfort bubble of the known and trusted, knowing that she might nonetheless feel under-challenged and that she has let herself and others down by not rising to the challenge of the new reframed job.

Reflective question

* How could coaching techniques be used to facilitate Katy in reconciling her ideal and actual selves?

are said to comprise ideal and also feared aspects. As Markus and Nurius (1986: 954) emphasise, a future self may depict an individual's 'ideas of what they might become, and what they are *afraid of becoming*' and as such project into the future one's goals and aspirations but also fears. Like goals, these imagined self-projections provide motivational and self-regulatory impetus.

A feared future self may, for example, create approach-avoidance dilemmas. For example, one may fear failure, which can either promote over-compensatory behaviour in relation to a desired goal (to minimise the likelihood of failure) and/or inhibit an individual from even entering an achievement domain that might threaten them with even the remotest possibility of failure. Fear of failure can also lead to procrastination, which is itself action disabling.

An ideal future self could on the other hand promote unrealistic strivings. This is most obviously seen among young people with aspirations to be rich and famous. On the surface, this aspiration may be fair enough but whether it is achievable is a different issue, and may lead to failure unless there has been some realistic pathway to success mapped out in advance. The point here is that through working with the concept of possible selves, a coach can facilitate realistic goal setting in a meaningful personal context of past, present and future considerations (Locke, 1968; Locke *et al.*, 1981; Locke and Latham, 1990).

Fundamentally, we also need to ask whether research has been too preoccupied with performance and thus neglected other outcomes of feedback. The effects of feedback on mood have been documented in a student sample (Kluger *et al.*, 1994), where a more pleasant mood is associated with good grades but also with whether these grades were expected, whereas arousal tends to tail off at a certain point. Note that mood also influences how we *give* feedback, as negative mood produces less polite and more negative feedback; this is particularly true for those with less experience (Forgas and Tehani, 2005). These observations have implications for coaching as coaches need to be cognisant of how their own mood affects their feedback style and to what extent the message is positive or negative. We provide an example in Text Box 4.4.

Text Box 4.4   Moods, emotions and feedback

Lesley, the coach, has been commissioned by the financial institution Big Bank to work with a senior manager, Will, on stress reduction techniques. Will missed the first session due to work commitments. Lesley feels irritated at this as they specifically agreed a time that would suit Will, meaning that Lesley had to shift appointments. In the next session, Lesley and Will agree to work on practical stress management techniques. Will seems distracted, and Lesley challenges him either to stop thinking about other things and start cooperating or to terminate the session there and then.

Reflective questions

- How could Lesley and Will deal with their emotions for the benefit of the coaching sessions and coaching relationship?
- To what extent is it necessary to make emotions explicit when using feedback?

Thus, the content of the feedback is important. Negative feedback is likely to provoke a whole host of downbeat reactions, such as hurt, anger, shame or sadness. Levels of distress will be more pronounced for individuals lacking in self-esteem (e.g. Brown and Dutton, 1995; Brown and Marshall, 2001). Bernichon *et al.* (2003) found that those high in self-esteem will seek feedback that verifies their self-view, even when this is negative, whereas those low in self-esteem will seek positive feedback, even if this is not congruent with their self-view.

Other individual characteristics also have a bearing on reactions to feedback. These include self-efficacy, locus of control and neuroticism, which taken together with self-esteem are referred to as self core evaluations (Judge *et al.*, 1997). These are clearly linked to both motivational characteristics such as self-determination (Judge and Hurst, 2007) as well as goal-setting strategies themselves (Erez and Judge, 2001), which we illustrate with another example in Text Box 4.5. This shows that someone high on neuroticism, whose self-efficacy in a particular performance domain is low, and with an external locus of control is likely to be less self-determined and more goal avoidant.

Text Box 4.5   Understanding individual differences

Julianne is in her late thirties and laments the fact that she has been bypassed for promotion on four occasions. She has initiated a series of sessions with an executive coach. Looking closely at her case, it would seem that she has become 'her own worst enemy'. First, Julianne expects to be promoted (external locus of control) and has not taken any proactive steps either to develop her self or to be known as someone who wishes to be promoted. Second, she is an anxious and nervous person (high neuroticism) and avoids situations that increase this anxiety, such as public speaking and chairing meetings, and says to her coach that she has been typecast as a 'wall flower'. Third, Julianne is low on self-perceived efficacy (the belief in her own capability) when it comes to dealing with people. Altogether, she has not done herself any favours.

Reflective questions

- How can a coach facilitate a situation in which Julianne receives 'feedback' on how she is seen by others and why she has been bypassed for promotion (i.e. 'mirror mirror on the wall, who am I in the eyes of others?')?
- How can the coach enable Julianne to start taking responsibility for how she presents herself, what she wants to become and how she is going to get there?

Feedforward

Having outlined theories that are mainly concerned with feeding back, so giving information on what has happened in the distant to immediate past, we acknowledge that there is also a more future-focused orientation. Feedforward is rooted in Positive Psychology (e.g. Seligman, 2000) and Appreciative Enquiry [AI] (Cooperrider and Srivastava, 1987). The basic tenets of AI are to use the best of 'what is' to pursue the possibilities of 'what could be' (Ashford and Parker: 4, cited in Willoughby and Tosey, 2007), taking a social construction-ist perspective, where realities emerge through communication and language. Emphasis is firmly on achievements, as opposed to problem solving, and on mutual participation. Kluger and Nir (2006) reasoned that AI, paired with the relatively recent movement of Positive Psychology, which also endeavours to promote the functional rather than inhibit the dysfunctional, offers a framework for optimising feedback processes – 'feedforward first, feedback later'. The authors argue that too much of our practice is concerned with the evaluation of past behaviour. Such practice is liable to a whole host of unwanted effects and distortions, such as biases where we rate those whom we like highly or placing more weight on a superior's rating even if this is wrong. Instead, it is more fruitful to put those who are about to receive feedback into a positive frame of mind first by focusing on strength, then getting them to think about the future before feeding back performance information. While controlled evidence for this model is extant at the time of writing, the underlying principles are widely accepted in the psychological community and we have used this to good effect in our own practice; see Text Box 4.6.

Text Box 4.6   Using 'feedforward'

The first author undertook an executive development programme where several senior managers were referred for individual feedback and coaching sessions, with the particular remit of coaching and facilitating progression potential to even senior ranks. Peter, a senior operations manager in his fifties, was initially presenting himself as reluctant, saying that 'he had always been a "thorn in the side of management", was by nature difficult to deal with and thus could not see how he could benefit'. The session thus concentrated on getting Peter to think about situations where he felt at his best, and then making plans for the future. This led to the realisation that Peter had little desire to grow into a senior role that involved more hands-on staff management, but would rather enhance his technical skills and become a recognised expert in the organisation. The last step was to agree an action plan that could be taken outside the coaching session, to be shared and agreed with other stakeholders in the organisation.

Reflective questions

- What do coaches need to be mindful of when using 'feedforward'?
- Can you think of situations where this technique would be more or less appropriate?

We note, however, that even 'feedforward', which puts much emphasis on how we should facilitate the recipient's positive frame of mind, has little to say about the mood and affect of the feedback giver, and how both parties can influence each other. These aspects need to be addressed by the coach in order to utilise the process to maximum effectiveness.

Effective goal setting in the coaching relationship

We posited earlier and showed in the example in Text Box 4.6 that coaching helps people to set more specific goals (Smither *et al.*, 2005) thus making the feedback process more effective. One lens for viewing and explaining these findings are self-regulatory theories of motivation such as Goal Setting Theory (Locke and Latham, 1990). These theories hold unique appeal for a coaching context. First, they posit 'human agency' – in other words, your world is what you make it. Second, goals are actionable and manipulated by managers (Vancouver and Day, 2005) or indeed coaches and coachees. The setting of more specific and difficult goals undeniably results in better performance (Locke and Latham, 2002). However, we lack rigorous experimental research that demonstrates the effectiveness of goal setting (Vancouver and Day, 2005). According to Possible Selves Theory (Markus and Ruvolo, 1989: 211), one must also invest in the goal for it to be a driver of action, that is, 'the crucial element of a goal is the representation of the individual herself and himself approaching and realising the goal. Without this representation of the self, a goal will not be an effective regulator of behaviour'. This argument aligns with findings that goals to which individuals are not committed are unlikely to be achieved (Locke and Latham, 1990). Thus, it is the 'I' (or self) that holds the goal and that gives self-relevant meaning, form and direction to the goal. As for any 'goal' to be successfully attained, the end-state (i.e. possible self) envisaged must be valued (i.e. important, invested with personal meaning) and must be coupled with a belief in its attainability. In this way, possible selves invest end-states with specific cognitive and/ or affective form, thereby facilitating the evolution of relevant plans and strategies for achieving them (Markus and Ruvolo, 1989). The implications for the coaching relationship are that coaches need to be mindful not to 'superimpose' what they think is the right goal for their coachees, but ensure buy-in and commitment throughout the process.

To assess the motivational impetus of goal setting within a Possible Selves framework, we conducted our own experimental study as outlined in Text Box 4.7.

Text Box 4.7   Goal setting studied as a group coaching intervention

Conventionally, 'goals' are represented simply as endpoints with little, if any, attention paid to their identity implications. We wanted to know what difference, if any, it might make if the goal is instead represented in the form of a 'possible self' rather than merely visualised at an entirely abstract level, thus servicing individuals with strategies for achieving such 'possible selves'.

Over 80 individuals from diverse occupations were recruited from an advert in a local newspaper offering free career seminars in exchange for the completion of pre- and post-intervention questionnaires. We compared the relative effectiveness of two interventions (standard goal setting or goals represented as possible selves), relative to a no-intervention control group (for enhancing career self-concept, motivation for personal change and sub-goal achievement) at four- and eight-month post-intervention intervals. We developed various exercises consistent with the theory. For instance, in the possible selves group, participants were encouraged to use visualisation techniques to articulate their goals and were helped to develop action plans. A content analysis of goals highlighted three main areas of concern: raising self-esteem, gaining promotion and more money, and getting a balance in life between work, family, friends and self, in other words directed towards intrinsic rather than extrinsic success. Our final analysis showed that the possible selves intervention was superior overall in its impact on various career variables and on self-reported goal achievement. This highlights that goals are more likely to be effective if invested with meaning that originates from the 'I'.

In contrast to the study outlined in Text Box 4.7, most research on goal setting has been conducted in controlled laboratory settings, with specific time-bound (i.e. proximal) goals with clearly identifiable (i.e. quantifiable), mostly singular outcomes. Practice in the field, however, is likely to differ. Goals may be of a largely qualitative (i.e. diffuse, fuzzy boundaries) and long-term (i.e. distal) and multiple kind, and real life rarely permits that individuals can concentrate on one thing at a time. In the 'field' study presented in Text Box 4.7, the goals established by participants were qualitative life-goals operating largely at the macro level rather than micro level of analysis and of the cross-impact kind (i.e. interdependently linked goals and sub-goals), thereby taking the goal-setting technique into a more nebulous 'subjective' realm. In such circumstances it is not possible to control for degree of goal specificity or goal difficulty, for example – factors that are also critical to our understanding of how goal setting works.

Altogether, these findings indicate the potential for goal-setting concepts and techniques to be imported with some success into the developmental and therefore coaching domain. However, the conditions under which goal setting will make a difference must be noted. In the study presented in Text Box 4.7, for instance, participants all sought career development advice/counselling, and had entered a period of 'self-revision'. Thus, they were in the right frame of mind to make the intervention effective. Next, participants were from the outset encouraged to set their own goals and anchor these not only directly in the work domain, but also across other areas of their lives, to examine potential cross-impact and ensure a 'reality check' regarding their feasibility of attainment. Last, we ensured that various goals were unpacked into a hierarchy of concrete criterion-based sub-goals against which shorter timescales could be mapped (Cropanzano *et al.*, 1995). This ensured that participants would focus on goal attainment, and not be in danger of 'losing' more proximal or long-term goals along the way. Thus, this research shows that traditional goal-setting principles, allied with concepts of identity and possible selves, in combination can add significantly more value to career development strategy built on goal setting alone. It can be argued here that making issues of self and identity salient, and 'explicitly' harnessing goal setting as a vehicle for achieving self-development/career goals, provides the goal-setting process with depth and meaning, and thus 'anchors' it within the 'I'.

Relating this back to feedback practice, it could be speculated that the individual who possesses a very clear and vivid image of where they want to be in terms of identity issues is also more likely to rely on self-referent feedback rather than knowledge of results in the extrinsic sense. Those with goals that are not integrated with identity (past, present and future) are, on the other hand, perhaps more reliant on the achievement of actual results to keep them motivated, something difficult to establish precisely in relation to long-term life-goals. Thus, coaches will do well to ascertain, through questioning and feedback, where coachees' identities and selves are located, in order to determine whether action is best directed towards the short versus long term, or towards learning through the task versus achievement of outcomes.

Conclusion

Feedback is more complex than it appears at first glance, but in this chapter we outlined how psychological theory and evidence offers guidance for how to 'hold up the feedback mirror' in the context of coaching. The mirror needs to be positioned right so that coach and coachee can benefit from the reflection. In order to facilitate good interpersonal relations, our above discussion results in the following recommendations for coaching practice with particular reference to the coach:

- Be aware that feedback can relate to both processes and content. Where content feedback is directed towards the self (i.e. the coachee), great care must be taken that this is appropriately pitched.
- Ensure that you understand the personal characteristics of the coachee
- Open up two-way dialogue.
- Develop the skills to pitch feedback at the right level

and ensure through checking and questioning that this is understood by all.
- Be conscious of your own moods and inclinations and realise how these affect any feedback process.
- Make goals meaningful and invested with 'selves' to ensure buy-in and sustained motivation.
- Strike the balance between feeding back important information and feeding forward into the future.

As feedback is by its nature reciprocal in the context of relationships the onus is also firmly on coachees to:

- engage with and participate in the feedback process;
- give the coach open and honest feedback on both content ('are we doing the right thing for me?') and process (which issues/strategies are working for me and to what extent?');
- be receptive to working on potential blind spots and raising self-awareness;
- ensure that goals are actively being worked on, even if the goal posts need changing in consultation with the coach.

We conclude that both parties need to have balanced input into and control of feedback processes in a sound coaching relationship.

Reflective questions

- To what extent is there a difference between process and content feedback?
- Why is it important to understand individual differences that may affect either coach or coachee or indeed both?
- How can we invest goals with personal meaning?
- When would you choose what: feeding back or feeding forward?

References

Bernichon, T., Cook, K.E. and Brown, J.D. (2003) Seeking self-evaluate feedback: the interactive role of global self-esteem and specific self-views. *Journal of Personality and Social Psychology*, 84: 194–204.

Brown, J.D. and Dutton, K.A. (1995) The thrill of victory, the complexity of defeat: self-esteem and people's emotional reactions to success and failure. *Journal of Personality and Social Psychology*, 68: 712–722.

Brown, J.D. and Marshall, M.A. (2001) Self-esteem and emotion: some thoughts about feelings. *Personality and Social Psychology Bulletin*, 27: 575–584.

Carver, C. and Scheier, M. (1981) *Attention and Self-Regulation: A Control Theory Approach to Human Behavior*. New York: Springer.

Cooperrider, D.L. and Srivastava, S. (1987) Appreciative inquiry in organizational life. *Research in Organizational Change and Development*, 1: 129–169.

Cropanzano, R., Citera, M. and Howes, J. (1995) Goal hierarchies and plan revision. *Motivation and Emotion*, 19: 77–93.

Erez, A. and Judge, T.A. (2001) Relationship of core self-evaluations to goal setting, motivation and performance. *Journal of Applied Psychology*, 86: 1270–1279.

Forgas, J.P. and Tehani, G. (2005) Affective influences on language use: mood effects on performance feedback by experts and novices. *Journal of Language and Social Psychology*, 24: 269–284.

Higgins, E.T. (1997) Beyond pleasure and pain. *American Psychologist*, 52: 1280–1300.

Judge, T.A. and Hurst, C. (2007) The benefits and possible costs of positive core self-evaluations: a review and agenda for future research. In D.L. Nelson and C. Cooper (eds) *Positive Organizational Behaviour*. London: Sage.

Judge, T.A., Locke, E.A. and Durham, C. (1997) The dispositional causes of job satisfaction: a core evaluations approach. *Research in Organisational Behaviour*, 19: 151–188.

Kluger, A.N. and DeNisi, A.S. (1996) The effects of feedback interventions on performance: a historical review, a meta-analysis, and a preliminary feedback. *Psychological Bulletin*, 119: 254–284.

Kluger, A.N. and Nir, D. (2006) Feedforward first – feedback later. Keynote address presented at the International Congress of Applied Psychology, Athens, July 2006.

Kluger, A.N., Lewinsohn, S. and Aiello, J.R. (1994) The influence of feedback on mood: linear effects on pleasantness and curvilinear effects on arousal. *Organizational Behavior and Human Decision Processes*, 60: 276–299.

Locke, E.A. (1986) *Generalizing from Laboratory to Field: Ecological Validity or Abstraction of Essential Elements?* Lexington, MA: Lexington Books.

Locke, E.A. and Latham, G.P. (1990) *A Theory of Goal Setting and Task Performance.* Englewood Cliffs, NJ: Prentice Hall.

Locke, E.A. and Latham, G.P. (2002) Building a practically useful theory of goal setting and task motivation. *American Psychologist,* 57: 705–715.

Locke, E.A., Shaw, K.N., Saari, L.M. and Latham, G.P. (1981) Goal setting and task performance. *Psychological Bulletin,* 90: 125–152.

London, M., Smither, J.W. and Adsit, D.J. (1997) Accountability: the Achilles' heel of multisource feedback. *Group & Organization Management,* 22: 162–184.

McDowall, A. (2008) Using feedback in coaching. In J. Passmore (ed.) *Psychometrics in Coaching.* London: Kogan Page.

Markus, H. and Nurius, P. (1986) Possible selves. *American Psychologist,* 41: 954–969.

Markus, H. and Ruvolo, A. (1989) Possible selves: personalized representations of goals. In L.A. Pervin (ed.) *Goal Concepts in Personality and Social Psychology.* Hillsdale, NJ: Erlbaum.

Seligman, M.E.P. (2000) The positive perspective. *The Gallup Review,* 3: 2–7.

Smither, J.W., London, W., Flautt, R., Vargas, Y. and Kucine, I. (2003) Can working with an executive coach improve multi-source feedback ratings over time? *Personnel Psychology,* 56: 23–44.

Smither, W., London, M. and Reilly, R.R. (2005) Does performance improve following multisource feedback? A theoretical model, meta-analysis, and review of empirical findings. *Personnel Psychology,* 58: 33–52.

Vancouver, J.B. and Day, D.V. (2005) Industrial and organisation research on self-regulation: from constructs to applications. *Applied Psychology: An International Review,* 54: 155–185.

Willoughby, G. and Tosey, P. (2007) Appreciative inquiry as a process for leading school improvement. *Educational Management Administration & Leadership,* 35: 499–520.

5

Assessment in coaching

Chris Smewing and Almuth McDowall

Introduction

As the focus of this book suggests, coaching is all about relationships and people issues. Yet it can be a curiously insular activity, which relies primarily on the interaction between coachee and coach, often without any external input. Thus, there is a potential danger of becoming overly reliant on opinions or perceptions held by those involved. Consider the scenario provided in Text Box 5.1.

Text Box 5.1   Coaching for leadership scenario

Sam, a business coach, has been commissioned by a large multinational client to coach Gemma, a senior sales manager. Sam asks Gemma about her goals for the forthcoming series of sessions. Gemma sees herself as an inspirational leader to the team, and would like to use the sessions to help her advance to a very senior role.

Reflective questions

- If you were Sam, would you use any assessments?
- If yes, which ones?
- What questions or hypotheses might you want to test out with the information from any assessments?

The use of assessment instruments can add an extra dimension to the coaching process, and provide a valuable source of information as well as the impetus for behaviour change. However, it is important that such instruments are used appropriately in order to avoid 'perceived' rather than actual objectivity and the reinforcement of inaccurate perceptions.

In this chapter, we begin by outlining different types of assessment, concentrating on the world of work. Next, we consider the results of a survey investigating the current usage of different assessment instruments in a coaching context. We then discuss the circumstances when assessment instruments should (or should not) be used. Following this, we outline how to use different assessments within the coaching process and, finally, future trends are considered. We illustrate our argument with figures and text boxes with examples or case studies (such as Text Box 5.1) to provide impetus for self-reflection to our readers.

Different types of assessment instruments

There are many different types of assessment instrument available, ranging from the objective, extremely reliable and well validated, to the subjective, based more on the intuition, creativity or wishful thinking of the coach. Some assessments focus on characteristics of the individual such as personality traits, attitudes, beliefs and values, whereas others are more task/action orientated. We provide an overview in Figure 5.1.[1] In the remainder of this section we consider (a) performance information, (b) aptitude/ability tests, (c) personality measures and (d) reflective tools or questionnaires such as the Life Balance Audit.

Performance information

Performance information refers to measures reporting how the individual actually carries out their work, or is perceived

[1] In this chapter we adopt a solutions-focused approach, and have therefore not included the many clinical measures available.

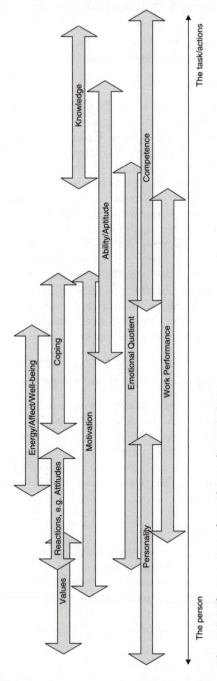

Figure 5.1 The person–task continuum in assessment

to do so, including performance data, performance appraisal and multi-rater (360-degree) assessment.

Actual performance data

The most objective type of performance information is historical data regarding actual achievements, outputs or results produced by individuals. Examples include the value or volume of sales made, progress towards productivity/utilisation targets or the quality of services provided. Such objective information can be valuable when used as part of the coaching process, particularly when performance is a key issue. For instance, when working with a coachee who has been referred due to derailment (so whose performance is falling below what is expected, or is even counterproductive) the information could provide the coach with a benchmark of performance, or even provide concrete data on the exact timings of performance changes, as we illustrate in Text Box 5.2. However, such information is not always readily available and generally becomes more difficult to obtain as job complexity increases and/or in service-orientated jobs.

Text Box 5.2   Coaching derailment scenario

Clive is a senior sales manager who has been leading a large multinational sales team for the last two years. His behaviour at work has become erratic over the last year and sales figures in his team are dropping. Natasha, an external executive coach, has been asked to coach Clive to improve his performance and personal relationships at work.

Reflective questions

• Should Natasha use assessments, and if yes, at what stage in the coaching process?
• What assessments might be useful, and what information could they bring to the coaching process?
• To what extent would the coach be the right person to obtain and interpret this information?

Coaches and coaching psychologists need to be aware of the following when using such information. First, a reasonable level of business awareness is needed to understand and discuss the information competently. Second, the data itself may not be as valid as it may seem. For example, it might not be a genuine reflection of actual performance, or might reduce complex tasks to a small number of 'key' indicators. Third, any discussion of performance data needs to be handled carefully to ensure that the coachee does not feel that he/she has to provide explanations/excuses for their performance rather than focusing on what he/she is going to do to improve.

Performance appraisal

Performance appraisals usually involve two elements: (a) the assessment of past performance (often based on competency frameworks) against clearly defined criteria that have been set in advance and (b) the setting of future objectives and goals (see Fletcher, 2001). They are implemented by most organisations in the UK, and are usually done once a year in a formal setting. Often, performance appraisals will include feedback, not just from the immediate boss, but also the line manager. Performance appraisal systems have grown in sophistication in recent years (see, for example, the balanced scorecard approach – Kaplan and Norton (1992) – or indeed the increased use of multi-rater assessments).

With regard to coaching, a performance appraisal report can provide coaches and coaching psychologists with details of the key objectives the individual is required to achieve, give an indication of their progress and, perhaps, some of the challenges they face, and give some insight into the relationship between the coachee and their boss.

There are, however, a number of potential challenges associated with using performance appraisal. The individual might be focusing on achieving their Key Performance Indicators irrespective of whether these are in the long-term interest of the organisation; thus, the big picture needs to be borne in mind, particularly when coaching has been commissioned by a client. Another issue is that the coach may not have access to, or wish to have access to, the assessors, and may therefore not fully appreciate the reasoning behind the assessments.

In the UK, a recent survey of 2,900 workers by Investors in People showed that 29 per cent of people felt that the experience of formal appraisals was a waste of time, and 44 per cent believed that the appraiser had been dishonest, while 41 per cent felt that overall the process was useful. These results highlight that appraisal information may not always be accurate, and that there can be a general lack of 'buy-in', particularly from the appraisees. For the coach, this has two implications. First, such information may not be correct and thus needs to be corroborated with the coachee and client. Second, it is feasible that the coachee may not have had any accurate or conducive appraisals of performance issues, which may underlie issues such as observed lack of confidence or self-insight.

Multi-rater (360-degree) assessment

Partly as a result of discontent with traditional appraisal systems, the use of multi-rater or 360-degree feedback has grown in recent years, facilitated by the development in online assessment instruments (commercially available products include Perspectives by Pearn-Kandola, Benchmarks® as published by OPP, or Multi-Rater Assessment by Cubiks).

In a full 360-degree audit, the individual concerned receives feedback from their manager and peers, and direct reports on various competencies. Additional key stakeholders such as other senior managers and even customers may be included. The individual also assesses themselves using the same dimensions and any gaps between self- and other assessments that are thought to facilitate learning and self insight (e.g. London and Smither, 1995). The exploration of these differences and resulting gap analysis is perhaps a key benefit of 360-degree assessments (McDowall and Kurz, 2008).

The wider benefits of using 360-degree assessments within a coaching context are that the individual is being assessed against indicators that the organisation believes to be important and they allow the comparison of different perceptions. The results of the assessment can be used to help coachees identify personal strengths and development needs in relation to required levels of performance. This, in turn, may lead to personal development/career planning.

By contrast, there are some who argue that 360-degree assessments are of little value, pointing to the subjectivity of the assessment process itself. Coaches need to be mindful of 'alternative agendas' and take extra care to corroborate feedback with the coachee, ensuring that competencies discussed are relevant to the respective job role (see McDowall and Kurz, 2008).

Aptitude/ability tests

The second major category of assessment instruments considers aptitude and ability.

Aptitude tests

Some aptitude tests demonstrate a person's ability to perform a particular type of task (e.g. a speed typing test for an administrator). Others may be more service orientated or leadership focused, such as executive in-tray exercises and case studies (see, for example, A & DC's AC-Ex range of products).

Within the coaching relationship, such measures can be very useful in helping the coach and coachee to identify and focus on specific aspects of a job that need improvement. They can also be useful for evaluating the impact of coaching engagement by measuring performance both prior to the commencement of coaching and at the end.

Coaches and coaching psychologists need to be mindful that while aptitude tests can provide a realistic indication of a person's ability in a particular area if they are appropriately chosen, they do not actually demonstrate what the person would do given a real-life situation.

Ability tests

There are a number of different types of ability test available, including verbal reasoning, numerical reasoning and spatial awareness (Kline, 1993). Ability tests are widely available, often easily administered and scored online, and many are well validated and reliable.[2] Ability tests can provide the coach with a fairly accurate indication of the ability of the coachee as measured by the test and help to further the coachee's understanding of their strengths and development needs but, again, they may not indicate how a person will actually respond in a real-life situation. In some circumstances, ability tests may also give insight into other behaviours such as bullying, which the coachee might resort to in order to compensate for their lack of ability in a particular area.

Personality measures

Personality questionnaires measure stable characteristics that underlie typical or preferred ways of behaving. These range from general measures linked to the Big Five personality dimensions (see below) to more specific aspects of personality such as conflict management, influencing style and innovation. We will therefore consider personality in somewhat more detail than previous sections. All of the tests mentioned below are validated, and are recognised as being 'satisfactory', by the British Psychological Society (please refer to the psychtesting website for reviews: www.psychtesting.org.uk).

General personality measures (including the 'Big Five')

The English language has more than 16,000 words to describe personality traits (Allport and Odbert, 1936). However, numerous studies have shown that the vast majority of these fall into five broad categories, namely openness, conscientiousness, extraversion, agreeableness and neuroticism (e.g. Goldberg, 1993). Together, they are referred to as the 'Big Five' and constitute the most widely accepted general model of personality used today.

---

[2]   For an extensive list of measures, visit the British Psychological Society, Psychological Testing Centre, www.psychtesting.org.uk

An example of an instrument that specifically measures the Big Five is the NEO Personality Inventory (Costa and McCrae, 1992). Others such as the OPQ32® (Bartram *et al.*, 2006) measure 32 dimensions of personality clustered around the Big Five. A more recent addition to the market is Saville Consulting's WAVE® model, which includes personal and focus styles, and although derived from the Big Five, identifies four main clusters (thought, adaptability, influence and delivery) subdivided into 36 categories (Kurz *et al.*, 2008).

Whereas WAVE Styles®, OPQ32® and NEO® all measure personality traits, the Meyers Briggs Type Indictor (MBTI®; Briggs Myers *et al.*, 1994) is designed to assess personality types. Personality types have been defined as 'distinct groups of people characterised by a unique configuration of features' (McCrae and Costa, 2003: 25). The test designers argue that there are 16 different types of personality, and that everyone will fall into one of these types. (It should be noted that Myers and Briggs do not claim that their instrument provides a complete summary of personality.)

The advantage of using one of the more traditional instruments such as the NEO® for coaching relationships is that the information provided is relatively parsimonious and easy to understand. The advantage of other tools such as the WAVE Styles® and OPQ32® is that they provide a more detailed feedback report that also taps into competence. While this granularity can be useful particularly when mapped against specific aspects of performance that need to be addressed through coaching, the onus is on the coach to make the information personal and meaningful.

Narrow Spectrum personality measures

There are also Narrow Spectrum instruments designed to measure very specific aspects of personality (Smith and Smith, 2005), which can be useful in getting the coachee to really consider particular aspects in some depth and increase awareness of alternative approaches. Just a few are listed below:

- creativity and problem-solving style: Kirton Adaptation-Innovation Inventory (Kirton, 2003);
- preferred team role: Belbin Team Roles Questionnaire (Belbin, 1996);
- learning style: Learning Styles Questionnaire (Honey and Mumford, 1986);
- leadership: Transformational Leadership Questionnaire (Alban-Metcalfe and Alimo-Metcalfe, 2007), now Engagement Leadership Questionnaire (ELQ));
- conflict resolution style: Thomas-Kilmann Conflict Mode Instrument (Thomas and Kilmann, 1974).

Personality measures can be useful in that they allow the coach to gain insight into the preferred behaviour of the coachee in a structured and systematic way, and provide insight into the coachee's perception of their own personality. As they are based on the coachee's self-assessment, personality measures may sometimes reinforce the coachee's self-perception, however, and make them less amenable to alternative perceptions. (We do acknowledge that some personality measures are now available in 360-degree format.) Furthermore, a growing number of online measures now have sophisticated response checks, which can identify systematic distortion by the respondent.

Reflective tools/life audits

The fourth category of assessment instruments consists of the plethora of questionnaires, exercises and tools designed to get an individual to reflect on some aspect of their career or even their life. We use the Life Balance Audit and the Timeline Satisfaction Indicator to illustrate this.

Life Balance Audit

This instrument can be used to help individuals to think about various aspects of their life at present. Categories might include family, friends, home environment, work/career, wealth, health, fun and hobbies and spiritual well-being (e.g. values and sense of purpose). For each category, the individual writes down what it is they like/appreciate,

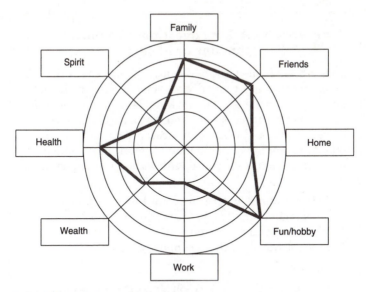

Figure 5.2 **Life Balance Audit example**

and what they are not satisfied with and wish to change. They may also rate their satisfaction with each category on a scale of 1 to 10 and plot these on a graph (see also Figure 5.2). This information can then be used as the basis of an action plan.

Timeline Satisfaction Indicator

This instrument, also sometimes called 'lifeline', is used to get an individual to reflect on significant events in their life and their relative impact. The individual begins by identifying any significant events that have had an impact on them in a given time period. Then, for each event, they rate themselves on some criteria such as happiness and plot this information on a timeline. In the example presented in Text Box 5.3, the individual has been asked to focus solely on their current job, but the instrument can be used to reflect on any period of time. The coach might use this information to formulate probing questions. Consider our example in Text Box 5.3, which relates directly to Figure 5.3.

Text Box 5.3   Asking questions around a timeline or lifeline

Jo is a team leader in a call centre. Think about the job demands that are typically associated with such roles, such as working shifts, working largely on the telephone, large shared offices and also a target and results driven culture. Jo has now presented for a series of coaching sessions to help manage work/life balance. In a coaching context, you might want to ask questions such as:

- Tell me about where on your line you felt at your peak. What happened that facilitated this?
- What was your contribution?
- In what way did others support you?

In addition:

- Would you also want to ask about the low points, and how could you phrase these questions?

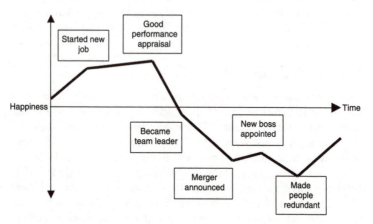

Figure 5.3 Timeline example

Tools such as those shown in Figures 5.2 and 5.3 are not validated in a psychometric sense, but nevertheless might provide a useful starting point for a coaching discussion, or add insight during the coaching process. They require the individual to reflect on some aspect of their life, or to consider what they want in the future, and they can encourage the coachee to identify areas that they had not focused on before. They also act as an 'external stimulus' that might draw out issues that otherwise the coach might be reluctant to discuss and which might bring increased honesty and openness to the coaching relationship.

Some of the criticisms of these types of tools are that they may be rather simplistic, that there is a lack of rigour in the way they are used and that there is very little research regarding the impact that they may have.

Which assessments do coaches actually use?

As there is little data available about what psychometric tools are used in activities other than employee selection, we conducted a survey to determine which ones are currently used in practice. The results were presented at the first European Coaching Conference (Smewing and McDowall, 2008).

We surveyed over 100 UK and international coaches regarding their use of assessments in coaching. Of our total sample, 88 per cent said that they used assessments, and most of those (60 per cent) said that they used them with at least 70 per cent of their coachees. Only 12 per cent of respondents said that they did not use assessments at all. The main reason given for this was that they did not feel that assessments 'added much value' (5 per cent). Of those who used assessments, the most popular reason was to 'open up areas for discussion' (Figure 5.4).

They open up areas for discussion	96.3%
They provide a useful source of data	79.3%
They are useful to my coachees	73.2%
They enable me to coach more effectively	48.8%
They provide structure to coaching sessions	41.5%

Figure 5.4 **Reasons for using assessments (90 respondents)**

Personality measures	86.3%
Multi-rater (360-degree) assessment/feedback	56.3%
Learning styles	35.0%
Emotional intelligence	32.5%
Interest questionnaires	31.3%
Performance data	26.3%
Intelligence/aptitude tests	20.0%
Competency measures	20.0%

Figure 5.5 **Types of measure used**

Personality questionnaires were the most widely used assessment instruments, followed by multi-rater (360-degree) assessment/feedback, and learning styles (see Figure 5.5).

With regard to specific measures used, the most popular was the Myers Briggs Type Indicator, followed by Shultz's Firo B/Firo Elements, and Cattell's 16PF/16PF5 (Figure 5.6).

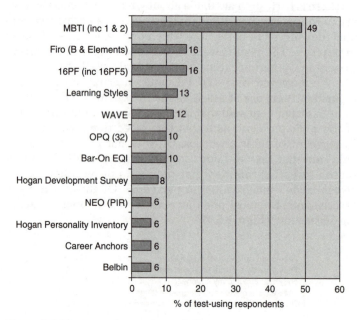

Figure 5.6 **Most popular measures (%)**

The main reasons why respondents chose a particular assessment instrument were because they were 'well researched and validated' (74.4 per cent), the coach was 'qualified to use them' (66.7 per cent), they were 'easy to use' (50.0 per cent) and because of the 'quality of reports produced' (48.7 per cent).

Thus, our survey indicates that assessment instruments are widely used as part of coaching, although they do not suit everybody. They are seen as providing useful information to both the coach and the coachee, and are also sometimes used to provide data to the client. While personality measures are the most popular, a wide range of different assessments are used, with some coaches using different assessments in different circumstances.

The rationale for using assessments

The wide range and easy availability of assessment instruments can make them very tempting to use, but coaches and coaching psychologists need to be clear as to why a particular instrument is being used, how it should it be used, what impact it might have on the coaching relationship and what the possible outcomes are.

One reason for using assessment instruments is to measure particular attributes of an individual (a profiling approach). Another is to predict a particular outcome (a criterion-orientated approach) (Passmore, 2007). Either approach can provide the coachee with information that can enable them to better understand their own personal characteristics, including strengths and weaknesses. In some circumstances, assessment instruments may increase individual self-awareness by identifying a particular characteristic or way of behaving that the coachee had not previously recognised or acknowledged.

Assessment instruments can also provide the coachee with a framework, model or language for discussing their own characteristics, and also give the coach a means for structuring one or several coaching sessions. While increased self-awareness for the coachee is desirable in itself, the next challenge for both the coach and the coachee is how best to make use of this new insight. To some extent this will be influenced by the type of coaching being undertaken. For example, within a work setting, a personality measure could help to highlight some of the challenges that an individual might face if they were to take on a new leadership role. This could lead to a discussion as to how the coachee may need to adapt their way of working in order to meet these challenges.

The use of assessment instruments in coaching can be very beneficial, but there are also a number of circumstances where they might be considered less appropriate. For example, if the coach and coachee are discussing a very personal issue, then an assessment instrument might be an unwanted distraction that disrupts the coaching discussion.

Each assessment instrument needs to be considered on its own merits and it is the responsibility of the coach to ensure that assessment instruments are only used for the purpose for which they were designed. For example, some work-specific personality measures are not suitable for use with young or inexperienced people as the actual items typically assume a certain level of work experience.

When to use assessment instruments in the coaching process

Once a coach has made the decision to use an assessment instrument within the coaching process, the next decision concerns when this should be introduced. Here we consider the differences in using them at the beginning, the middle or the end of the coaching process, providing an overview in Figure 5.7.

Assessments thus have various functions at different stages in the coaching cycle. In the beginning, they provide context and structure and also information about whether the relationship might work. During the process, specific assessments come into their own, particularly when a plateau or impasse has occurred. Lastly, they can be used to evaluate behaviour changes but also the process itself. Naturally, assessments could be deployed at all of these stages but coaches would need to be mindful not to over-assess or overload the coachee.

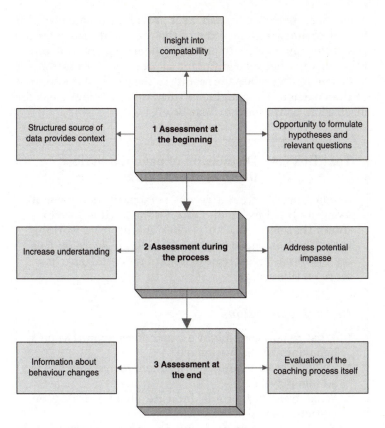

Figure 5.7 When to use assessments in coaching

How to use assessment instruments

A growing number of organisations now offer assessment instruments that can be completed online and that produce sophisticated reports. Some reports are designed in such a way that they can be given to the individual concerned and will make sense to them. However, a number of publishers stipulate that their instrument should only be used by a trained and experienced practitioner who can explain it to the individual concerned and explore the results with them. From a coaching perspective, there is much merit in this approach, as it provides the coachee with the opportunity to query any of the results. It also gives the coach the opportunity to provide a richer explanation of the relationships between different aspects of the assessment instrument, and relate the results to the particular situation of the coachee. This might, in turn, open up new areas for discussion, as we show in Text Box 5.4.

Text Box 5.4 Discussion of psychometric profiles in coaching

Lynda's profile from a recent personality assessment using a 'Big Five' tool – the Orpheus (Rust, 1996) – shows that she tends to get her energy from working with others in the workplace (so a 'high' score on this scale) but has an extreme disregard for detail (so a 'low' score on this scale).

Reflective questions

- What hypotheses might a coach form about Lynda's behaviour in the workplace?
- To what extent would her profile indicate that she is a team player?
- What does her profile indicate about working on meticulous tasks?
- Would you want to bring in any other types of assessment to understand and discuss this profile?

In order for the coach to feed back the data appropriately, she must understand the instrument, and be fully conversant with it. With regard to a personality measure, for example, it is essential that the coach has a clear understanding of the scale definitions that are used, and an appreciation of the linkages between them.

If the coach does choose to feed back the results to the coachee, they can present these either as a 'matter of fact' or as a series of hypotheses for further discussion. The approach taken will, in part, be determined by the assessment instrument used but also by the nature and purpose of the coaching sessions. In general, ability tests are considered objective, and it is therefore difficult to dispute the results. By contrast, personality measures are less objective, and may be more open to influence by other factors such as the mood of the coachee when they completed the questionnaire.

There are three main ways in which a coach can feed back the results of an assessment. One way is to go through each aspect of the questionnaire in turn, explain the results produced, and then ask for feedback from the coachee. Another option is to look for linkages and patterns within the data and identify broad themes for discussion with the coachee. This approach has the advantage of providing more of a coherent picture to the coachee, but can be difficult to do, especially if there are a lot of interwoven themes. A third option is to talk to the coachee about a topic that concerns them but then feed in the results of the assessment as appropriate. The information from the profile itself can also be useful to inform the style the coach uses when feeding back the results. To illustrate, a coachee who is highly detail conscious might appreciate the first approach, which facilitates a very detailed and in-depth discussion. However, the coach might need to be careful that this does not result in 'information overload'.

Summary of assessment advantages and disadvantages

In this section we summarise the advantages and disadvantages of using assessment instruments within the coaching process, which we list in Table 5.1.

We note that the usefulness of assessment is further dependent on skilful administration, the understanding of the coach and appropriate response checks (to address distortion).

In summary, then, assessment instruments are with us. They can be a useful source of information, and can add insight to the coaching process at various stages when used correctly and thus enhance the coaching relationship by introducing robust sources of information and structure for

Table 5.1 Advantages and disadvantages of using assessments

Advantages. Assessments can:	Disadvantages. Assessments can:
• bring additional information to the coaching relationship	• trigger 'assessment overload'
• provide a model or framework and structure	• distract from the key focus of discussion
• enable feedback from other people to be incorporated into the coaching interaction	• be reliant on feedback that is distorted or inaccurate
• offer objective data regarding performance	• produce inaccurate, unreliable or invalid data
• facilitate checking of progress against certain objectives	• be inadequate for addressing the issue that is being coached
• indicate changes in behaviour	• provide an excuse for the coachee's behaviour

conversation and questioning. We note that the easy availability of measures online renders them tempting to use, but the coaching community needs to be skilful at distinguishing between the good, the bad and the ugly. There has been little research regarding the use of assessments in coaching, and this is something that clearly needs to be addressed. While test publishers will contribute to this, there is a real need for independent research on topics such as:

• the validity and reliability of individual measures;
• the process by which such measures are used;
• the impact that assessments have on the coaching process and relationships;
• the outcomes of such measures;
• the compatibility of specific assessment instruments with particular coaching approaches.

If an assessment instrument is to be used as part of the coaching process, it is essential that the coach maintains the same high standards in choosing, administering and feeding back that instrument as they would bring to the rest of the coaching process. In fact, coaches can make a significant contribution to our understanding of these instruments by carrying out their own research at a local level by asking their coachees how useful they found particular instruments, and why this was so. We lament the demise of case study research in psychology and related disciplines as the sharing of such research on this topic with the coaching community is likely to greatly enhance our understanding.

Reflective questions

- Is an assessment the right tool to use for this coachee, at this stage in the coaching process?
- What assessments can the coach use given their expertise and training?
- Is the coach the best person to use and interpret this assessment information?
- At what stages in the coaching process does an assessment take which function?
- How can the coach best interpret and discuss the assessment information with the coachee, keeping a balance between objectivity and insight?
- How can the coach ensure that any assessment is not interpreted in an inappropriately subjective way depending on the coach's own preconceptions?
- How do all of the above impact on relationships in coaching?

References

Alban-Metcalfe, J. and Alimo-Metcalfe, B. (2007) The development of the private sector version of the (Engaging) Transformational Leadership Questionnaire (ELQ). *Leadership & Organisational Development Journal*, 28: 104–121.

Allport, G. and Odbert, H. (1936) Trait names: a psycholexical study. *Psychological Monographs*, 47: 1.

Bartram, D., Brown, A., Fleck, S., Inceoglu, I. and Ward, K. (2006) *OPQ32 Technical Manual*. Thames Ditton: SHL Group.

Belbin, R.M. (1996) *Team Roles at Work*. London: Butterworth-Heinemann.

Briggs Myers, I., McCaulley, M., Quenk, N. and Hammer, I. (1994) *MBTI Manual: A Guide to the Development and Use of the Myers Briggs Type Indicator* (3rd ed.). Palo-Alto, CA: Consulting Psychologist Press.

Costa, P. and McCrae, R. (1992) *NEO PI-R Professional Manual.* Odessa, FL: Psychological Assessment Resources, Inc.

Fletcher, C. (2001) Performance appraisal and management: the developing research agenda. *Journal of Occupational and Organizational Psychology*, 74: 473–487.

Goldberg, L. (1993) The structure of phenotypic personality traits. *American Psychologist*, 48: 34.

Honey, P. and Mumford, A. (1986) *Manual of Learning Styles.* Maidenhead: Honey Publications.

Kaplan, R. and Norton, D. (1992) The balanced scorecard – measures that drive performance. *Harvard Business Review*, 70: 71–79.

Kirton, M. (2003) *Adaptation-Innovation in the Context of Diversity and Change.* London: Routledge.

Kline, P. (1993) *The Handbook of Psychological Testing.* London: Routledge.

Kurz, R., McIver, R. and Saville, P. (2008) Coaching with Saville Consulting WAVE. In J. Passmore (ed.) *Psychometrics in Coaching.* London: Kogan Page.

London, M. and Smither, J. (1995) Can multisource feedback change perceptions of goal accomplishment, self-evaluations, and performance-related outcomes? Theory-based applications and directions for research. *Personnel Psychology*, 48: 803–839.

McDowall, A. and Kurz, R. (2008) Effective integration of 360 degree feedback into the coaching process. *The Coaching Psychologist*, 4: 7–19.

McCrae, R. and Costa, P. (2003) *Personality in Adulthood: A Five-Factor Theory Perspective* (2nd ed.) New York: Guilford Press.

Passmore, J. (2007) Using psychometrics and psychological tools in coaching. *Selection and Development Review*, 23: 3–7.

Rust, Y. (1996) *Orpheus Manual*, Pearson Assessment, London.

Smewing, C. and McDowall, A. (2008) What assessments do coaches use in their practice and why? *Proceedings of the First European Coaching Psychology Conference*. London: British Psychological Society.

Thomas, K. and Kilmann, R. (1974) *Thomas-Kilmann Conflict MODE Instrument.* Mountain View, CA: Xicom and CPP.

Recommended books

Kline, P. (1993) *The Handbook of Psychological Testing.* London: Routledge.

Passmore, J. (ed.) (2008) *Psychometrics in Coaching.* London: Kogan Page.

6

Reflexive coaching: linking meaning and action in the leadership system

Christine Oliver

Introduction

This chapter will take a systemic approach to the coaching relationship and task. The relevance of a systemic orientation, a framework for understanding and methodological tools will be outlined and then applied to a case where an executive struggled with a leadership challenge. It is proposed that an understanding of theory enables a depth and breadth of practice, facilitating a second-order approach to coaching whereby beliefs, assumptions and expectations about organizational interaction can be linked to leadership behaviour. This approach contrasts with coaching accounts that emphasize technique disconnected from theory. The account is aimed to facilitate the ability to make sense of and intervene in patterns of communication, both in the coaching relationship and in leadership conversations for the coachee. A core skill of *reflexive agency* will be highlighted as crucial to the work of coaching, where the aim is to help the coachee develop productive patterns with those in his or her network of business concern, conversation and relationship. This network can be thought of as the *communication system*.

A systemic orientation to coaching

The notion of system in the organizational literature has taken different forms (Pearce, 2007). It is used here to mean a focus on patterns of connection in communication – the patterns of our behaviour with others and the meanings we individually and collectively make of that experience (Bateson, 1972). The word 'science' etymologically means 'to cut' and conventionally the focus of science has been to separate out parts and analyse them. A systemic approach involves a paradigmatic shift from the 'conventional', inviting us to look for the relationships among the parts and the contexts they set for making meaning and deciding action. Inspired by and adapted from Systemic Family Therapy (Burnham, 1986; Cecchin *et al.*, 1987; Dallos and Draper, 2005), systemic organizational approaches have drawn on Communication Theory (Cronen and Pearce, 1985; Barge and Oliver, 2003; Oliver, 2005) and Social Constructionist Theory (Campbell, 2000) to develop frameworks and tools to enrich organizational understanding and effectiveness, from the perspectives of both organizational participants and consultants. This chapter will apply that understanding to the work of the coach.

This approach emphasizes how communication is the medium through which we construct experience, knowledge, identity, relationship and culture. Language is treated less as a *representation* of reality and more as holding potential for *constructing* organizational realities. Communication, in these terms, is always unfinished but through conversation we create provisional boundaries around meaning. We become interested in the recursive relationship between how people live out their conversations in the organization and how narratives are facilitated to structure experience that fit and develop organizational purposes and visions. Since language is treated as significant, the interest develops as to how such narratives shape possibilities for effective action, for individuals and for the organization. The focus becomes conversation as performance, with the leader in a key legitimized role of influence.

In O'Neill's (2007: 5) terms the executive has four core tasks: mapping the territory of the task for his or her team; building relationships and team performance; producing direct outcomes from his or her own efforts; and facilitating the efforts of others. Conversation thus takes on a moral dimension because through its medium, leaders are positioned to facilitate or inhibit powers for self and others to act and, from this perspective, obliged to develop reflexive skills in noticing their assumptions and the effects of their behaviour. A coach, with the aim of facilitating *reflexive agency*, encourages a coachee to make conscious, situated choices and decisions that reflect and develop the complexity of business contexts that are being acted out of and into. Through connecting the contextual parts of a system, reflexivity is facilitated for leadership action. Van der Haar and Hosking (2004) distinguish constructivist from constructionist approaches to reflexivity. In the former, reflexivity is an intra-cognitive activity of an individual inquirer who separates him/herself from his/her own discourse, examining his/her own assumptions, similar to a metacognitive capacity. In contrast, a constructionist approach to reflexivity is socio-relational and focuses attention on processes of relating, with the inquirer seen as a participant in the discourse that s/he is co-constructing (Oliver, 2005; Oliver *et al.*, 2008). The systemically oriented coach will incorporate both approaches to reflexivity and work to encourage *reflexive agency* for and with the coachee. A framework for understanding the detailed focus for systemic curiosity and reflexivity will be articulated next.

A framework for understanding

Within the systemic field, interconnecting parts of a system are often thought of in terms of people and relationships. O'Neill (2007: 13), for instance, in a recent book offering a systems approach to coaching, advocates that the executive coach focuses on 'the system of human beings caught in a dilemma', but her framework for what counts as a system, represented in nested spheres moving from leadership traits and motivations to strategic alliances, global environment and economy, is a little loose and imprecise. She acknowledges the lack of fluidity in the model. My observation is that there is a conceptual confusion in O'Neill's model, drawing insufficient distinction between the map and the territory. In other words, how are experiences and the narratives about those experiences distinguished and connected?

The word 'system' is used here to define the connections and distinctions between our *patterns* of experience and our *narratives* about those experiences. The *communication system* in focus for the coach and coachee, from this perspective, is the recursive relationship among an interconnecting network of experiences and narratives that relate to the coachee's sphere of leadership influence. These categories need greater elaboration.

Cronen and Pearce (1985), working to connect social constructionist and systemic theory and practice, develop a conceptualization of context and meaning in their work on Coordinated Management of Meaning Theory. They propose that contexts are multiple, multilayered and in circular relationship. From contextual experiences we construct contextual narratives from which to interpret future experiences. The framing or narrative of a context shapes the way that meaning in a communication episode is interpreted, influencing emotional and behavioural responses, which in their turn influence the experience and framing of contexts. While any context could be of influence, the contexts most likely to influence organizational and leadership narratives and patterns of behaviour are those of the wider business environment, organizational culture, relationship, identity and task definition. Further, the situational details of any leadership episode will give clues for making meaning and action. The coachee will be affected by what has gone immediately before in a leadership communication and expectations about what will follow. Thus, the coachee's meaning-making and decision-making abilities are shaped by social processes, as are his/her ability to act with *reflexive agency*. Coaching, as another social process, can facilitate development of these abilities.

Cronen and Pearce develop a vocabulary for considering our *responsibilities* for the ways we make meaning and take action. They point out that the contexts that shape meaning and action carry with them 'rules' for what counts as legitimate, obligatory, entitled and forbidden. For instance, a leader may feel that it is appropriate to critique a subordinate's performance in the context of his or her obligations to the individual, the team and the organization, but may feel less entitled to critique a peer if there is no legitimized culture or structure for such behaviour. These ways of constructing social reality will have been influenced by the contexts invoked above (and maybe others) and the ways that he or she takes up his/her responsibility for action will implicate future definitions and experience of task, identity, relationship and culture for self and other(s) in the *communication system* (see Figure 6.1). Cronen and Pearce advocate that it is helpful in understanding communication to consider what context is having the strongest influence in any given situation and how the contexts of influence relate to each other, to the episode and to the interaction in the episode.

In a previous book Oliver (2005) develops this model and introduces the notion of the *interpretive act* as a metaphorical place or space for exercising responsible reflexivity. Through this mechanism, reflexive consideration is invited of one's own and others' contextual narratives influencing communication episodes, our emotional responses to a communication, the meanings made of it, particularly in terms of what kinds of rules are invoked, the imagined purposes of the next action, the choices that are possible and the behavioural decision, which then invites a response in turn from others in the system. In responding, we position others with opportunities and constraints to act. For instance, if a leader contextualizes an act of critique of a subordinate's performance with the statement, 'I want to facilitate development of this particular aspect of your performance', it is

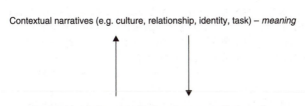

Contextual narratives (e.g. culture, relationship, identity, task) – *meaning*

Contextual experiences (episodes of communication) – *action*

***Figure 6.1* Leadership communication system**

more likely that the subordinate will be clearer about the leader's intentions and aims and respond favourably than if the critique had been made without contextualization. The interpretive act is shaped by a multiplicity of contexts as described above, and, in turn, shapes and reshapes further contexts for influencing emotion, meaning and action, identity, relationship and culture.

The *interpretive act* is broken down into three parts: emotional response, interpretation and action. This is not to suggest that these are separate dimensions of a response in any crude linear sense but only that they are useful lenses from which to examine the observations, interpretations and choices one makes in a leadership communicative episode. Through amplifying the detail of the *interpretive act* in this way, the potential for *reflexive evaluation* is increased when one can become more conscious of the partiality and multiplicity of possibilities for interpretation and action.

Emotional response: at the point of receiving a communication, we are helped or hindered by our emotional responses in interpreting it. These responses are coloured by contextual experiences and narratives, both personal and professional. They are inevitably partial, both in the sense that we can never notice all there is to be noticed and in the sense that our contextual experiences can only provide us with a partial lens. The staff member whose performance has been critiqued may feel supported or stressed or have other feelings, depending on his/her relationship with the leader, the culture of the organization and other contextual experiences and the narratives that emerge from them.

Interpretive response: our emotional responses contribute to meaning making at the interpretive level. In addition, our personal and professional contextual experiences and narratives tend to create habitual *rules for interpretation*, which we draw on in leadership communication episodes. However, we can exercise conscious choice in interpreting and reflecting on our interpretations. We can frame the same episode of communication in many different ways, thereby unpacking the multiplicity of meanings that have potentially been conveyed. Reframing meaning where useful is a reflexive ability that can generate new contexts for action. It is important to imagine what interpretation(s) best empower one's own response (and the potential for others to respond in their turn) in ways that develop leadership purposes and effectiveness.

To illustrate, the leader may interpret his team member's reluctance to accept critique as further evidence of poor performance, which could lead him to critique further. However, his mode of feedback may shape the responses of the team member considerably, inviting an interpretation from the staff member of 'personal attack', and requires reflexive consideration from the leader.

Action: our interpretation(s) of our own and another's meaning, motivation and purpose will shape the decision we make to act (i.e. the next move in the conversation) and influence whether our decisions to act have a *reactive* or *reflexive* quality. We tend to invoke habitual *rules for action*, which are shaped by layers of contextual experience and current contexts of influence and manifested in what our emotions and interpretations tell us.

To illustrate, the *rule for action* that could be invoked for the leader in this case might be 'when faced with unresponsive behaviour from a subordinate, I must retrieve power by showing my authority'. Thus, a mutually reinforcing reactive pattern can be maintained, developed or transformed, depending on the conscious (or reflexive) choices made by the participants. Interpretive acts become patterns over time. In drawing attention to the reflexive opportunities in a communication, the aim is to encourage conscious purposeful communication and to develop effective patterns of leadership and team action through encouraging a reflexive relationship to past, present and anticipated future patterns (see Figure 6.2).

This chapter, in reflecting on a particular coaching episode, will link hypotheses about contexts of influence to the interpretive acts of the coachee in his working context. A key moment is defined as one where the choice point in the interpretive act is felt to be crucial in determining future

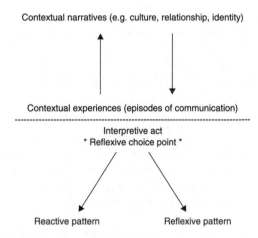

Contextual narratives (e.g. culture, relationship, identity)

Contextual experiences (episodes of communication)

Interpretive act
* Reflexive choice point *

Reactive pattern   Reflexive pattern

Figure 6.2 **Reflexive Leadership Model**

contexts, either by reinforcing an unwanted reactive pattern or by providing opportunities for shaping a desired new reflexive pattern for the leadership system. Such moments are decided through an ongoing process of observation and hypothesizing about the links between contexts, patterns and interpretive acts within the leadership *communication system* and the coaching system.

Systemic methodological tools

A systemic orientation to coaching highlights the detail of coach/coachee conversation as a core site of interest and as the place for analysis and the beginnings of change. Thus, conversation is seen as holding the power to make or break leadership patterns and narratives. The framework of thinking offered so far stimulates the production of concrete tools for helping us to coordinate our thinking and action in conversation with those we coach. These tools are best described as forms of inquiry, reflection and formulation. Following formulation, the opportunity for decision for action is created. Coaching thus becomes a cycle of inquiry, reflection, formulation and decision.

Inquiry

The systemic tradition has made a unique contribution to inquiry methodologies through its writings on circular and reflexive questioning (Penn, 1985; Cecchin *et al.*, 1987; Tomm, 1987). The origins of the approach are in systemic psychotherapy, but the principles and patterns of questioning can be developed in a coaching context, both one to one and in a group setting. Inquiry is not treated as prior to action but *as* action in the sense that narratives and patterns can be maintained or challenged through the ways that questions are posed or language is framed. The coach from this position asks him or her self – *what kind of development am I making possible through my intervention?* All communications from the coach are thought to have power for maintenance of or challenge to the leadership system in the ways they encourage or discourage reflexive leadership.

Different writers have offered a variety of categorizations for inquiry (Penn, 1982; Tomm, 1985). Figures 6.3 and 6.4

Context	Culture	Relationship	Identity
Self	How does the team *culture* provide possibilities for open and specific feedback and how do you influence that culture as leader?	In this *relationship*, where do you experience clarity and where is there confusion in your understanding of when it is appropriate to critique and when it is appropriate to offer some other form of leadership intervention?	When did you first experience *yourself* as finding critique a challenge with this particular member of your team? What might this say about your ideas about what counts as good leadership?
Other(s)	How might the team member describe significant *cultural* patterns in the organization that affect the ways he feels able to relate to you as leader?	How might the team member say you respond to his feedback to you on the impact of your leadership on the *relationship* and his ability to perform?	How might the team member describe his *role* and task?

Figure 6.3 Reflexive Leadership Model: inquiry into contextual narratives

Context	Emotion	Interpretation	Action
Self	When you received x communication from the team member, what did you feel? Have you felt that before in the team? What effect does your emotional response have on your ability to act? When have you noticed a different feeling?	How do feelings connect to thoughts? What choice do you have in how you are interpreting the situation? Where does your sense of obligation come from? How did your stories about the relationship affect the way you interpreted it?	How did your interpretation shape your action? When you act in that way, how does it affect the team member? What would you like to create? What new interpretation could enable different action? What interaction could help the organization?
Other(s)	What did you notice about your team member's body language? How did that affect your response? How might the cultural pressures in the organization have shaped his feelings? If he were more open about his feelings, how might you be affected?	If you thought of him as vulnerable and acting out of a sense of obligation, how would you make sense of what happened? How do you think he interpreted your response? What choices might you say he had in his response?	How did your subordinate respond to your response? Was that the response you hoped for? How might you have acted differently if you felt you had more choice in creating the response that was best for the relationship (and the organization)?

Figure 6.4 **Reflexive Leadership Model: inquiry into the interpretive act**

show the kinds of questions that can be useful in generating reflexive leadership action in a coaching context, referencing relevant contexts implied by the *Reflexive Leadership Model* to structure questions. These examples of questions represent a fraction of the potential for inquiry in a given situation. The example of critique of a team member is used to illustrate. Questions are focused on the coachee's experience (self) and the coachee's observations of the team member's experience (other), to enhance an observer perspective and encourage a distancing to 'fixed' reactive patterns. Questions are framed from a stance of 'authoritative doubt' (Mason, 2005), facilitating the 'right answer' to come from the coachee, not assumed by the coach. A spirit of 'discovery' is conveyed in the context of a questioning of taken-for-granted 'realities'. Taking a social constructionist position, 'realities' are assumed to be temporary, partial and emergent (Oliver, 2005).

Reflection

Elkjaer (2001: 440), writing about the learning organization, describes how John Dewey, the American pragmatist, connected reflection processes with situated learning processes. Reflection, he argues, works creatively when it allows for inquiry into *situations of uncertainty*. He suggests that meaning is created when connections are made between experience and its consequences. Learning develops when those meanings are linked to present concerns. This connects with O'Neill's (2007) point that coaching is a conversation about conversations about leadership *challenges*.

From a systemic perspective, a reflective position in coaching is one that aims to encourage such learning through facilitating the development of the reflexive relationship of the coachee to his or her own behaviour, emotion, interpretation and contextual narratives and their effects on the leadership system. Raelin (2001: 11) also argues for reflection as a basis for learning: 'Reflection is the practice of . . . stepping back to ponder the meaning to self and others in one's immediate environment about what has recently transpired'. In Raelin's terms, the coach can facilitate three levels of reflection on leadership and/or the coaching experience: *content* (what can be learnt from what happened?); *process* (what can be learnt from how it happened?); and *premise* (what beliefs and assumptions influenced what happened?). This triangle is a helpful structure to assist in developing reflexive leadership. In this chapter, the language of contextual narratives relates to the notion of premise; action will relate to content; and patterns of emotion, interpretation and action will relate to process.

Oliver proposes that reflection within coaching facilitates meta-communicative learning, i.e. learning about learning. Its benefits can be multi-levelled but in any given circumstance will have a specified focus and aim. The learning potential developed may be at levels of organizational culture, relationship and/or identity. At a cultural level, regular reflection practices can help to enhance a community of practice, challenging and enhancing cultural patterns and narratives (Lave and Wenger, 1991). At a relational level, learning can occur about patterns of communication and effective processes developed. At an individual level, meaning can be opened up so that interpretive acts can be connected to social processes and narratives enriched through building patterns of connection.

One important source for inspiring reflection is the systemic psychotherapy tradition where particular rules have been developed to facilitate the opening up of meaning and the preservation and enhancement of the dignity of participants in a session. A reflection takes the form of a hypothesizing conversation about a conversation, where conscious links begin to get made. In the psychotherapy context, the therapist's team speak about the conversation the therapist has been having with the client, in front of the therapist and client(s) (Andersen, 1991). The conversation between therapist and client(s) then resumes, linking back to the reflection. In a coaching context, reflection can be used as a means to enhance dialogue, learning, leadership practices and relationships through the same means of a conversation about a conversation. This can be applied to the conversations within the leadership *communication system* and/or to the coaching conversations themselves, facilitating meta-communication. Reflection allows the coach to step out of the inquiry position and to collaborate with the coachee in explicit hypothesizing about the dilemmas or uncertainties faced. Alternatively, some coaches working from a systemic perspective work in pairs and reflect in front of the coachee, who is then in a position to select the best of the reflected ideas presented. The added benefit of this structure is that the coachee, when placed in the third-person position, is released from the obligation to respond immediately, which is normally invoked in dialogue between first and second persons. The guidelines developed in the psychotherapy context are expanded below to fit a coaching context. They are linked to the coaching example that has been developed so far.

Guidelines for reflecting conversations

- Decide the *focus* for reflection, e.g. the obligations and entitlements imagined for leader and team member and how they link to contextual narratives.
- Decide how to *position* participants as speakers and listeners, e.g. coach and coachee, following an inquiry process, could then reflect on aspects of the material produced together, thus taking more of an observer position to the material.
- Position speakers and listeners in the reflection with a clear *purpose*, e.g. to reflect on cultural and team patterns that shape the pattern of the relationship in order to help to make sense of the pattern.
- Assume that the coachee behaves as he or she does because he or she is lacking systemic information and needs to make links previously not made.
- Act reflexively, mindful of the effects of the use of verbal and non-verbal language on coachee motivation and identity.

Formulation

The linking of contextual narratives and contextual experience will begin in the coaching session but is always emergent and open to new shaping as new information is created. However, it is the coach's responsibility to create punctuations of clarity to facilitate new forms of thinking and behaviour. Such linkages may occur in-between sessions and are part of the ongoing coaching narrative.

Decision

The task of decision is for the coachee; the role of the coach is to *facilitate* appropriate and creative decisions for action. Potential interventions will be at the level of either meaning (contextual narrative) or action (contextual experience). In other words, the coachee may decide to explore, develop or challenge his or others' narratives about their experience or may actually try to do something differently within experience. The latter may include exiting a pattern or constructing a reflexive pattern, however, continuing a pattern may also be good judgement once all relevant contexts are taken into account. Continuing a pattern for wider contextual reasons in a context of self-awareness will invariably change the dynamic and outcome as consciousness facilitates choice.

Case study

This illustration, adapted from the coaching practice of Business Therapy (Oliver Clarke, 2010) will attempt to show some links between inquiry, formulation and decision. The example is from a coaching session with Bart, head of research in a credit management company (CMC). The senior management team has five members, two of whom are co-founders and chief executives of the company and own a greater proportion of shares. Bart's role is to mediate and coordinate activity between traders and researchers in the company. In an early coaching session, Bart shared how challenging he experienced his role. He was also concerned about how one of the chief executives treated him. He felt undermined by his dismissive and aggressive behaviour. Traders and researchers were in a conflicted and competitive dynamic with each side disqualifying the other through their behaviour. This dynamic undermined the potential for creative outcomes. Bart found that much of his time was spent attempting to pacify either 'side' and/or overcompensating for his identification with the researchers by supporting the traders. He found it very hard to maintain a grounded leadership position, with sufficient leverage for effective leadership action.

Inquiry

Some key questions were asked in an attempt to explore links between contextual narratives and experience (see Figure 6.5).

Context	Culture	Relationship	Identity
Self	How does the culture of the business environment encourage or discourage appropriate competition and collaboration? How does your behaviour support or challenge that culture?	How does the relationship of the chief executives shape communication possibilities within the CMC? What is their perception of how you enact your role?	How does the perception of the chief executives shape your perception of your abilities as leader? If you felt more confident, how might that show itself in your behaviour and how might that affect the relationship between traders and researchers?
Other(s)	What culture is created through the way the leadership team relates to the chief executives and what would be their perspectives on the culture created?	How would you describe team motivation and morale? How is this affected by the relational pattern between the chief executives?	What does the chief executive do to influence your feeling undermined? What do you imagine are the pressures for the chief executive you find difficult? What do you imagine has influenced his pattern of leadership?

Figure 6.5 **Case example**

Reflection

The inquiry produced some responses, which coach and coachee reflected upon. It emerged that Bart felt that he was in an oscillating, unstable pattern with the chief executives, whereby in one episode he would feel micro-managed and in the next he would feel abandoned, interpreting their treatment of him as bullying yet feeling no entitlement to comment on the pattern. This had the effect on him of feeling like giving up at times but, at other times, feeling anxiously connected to work. This reinforced a feeling of insecurity, yet he had felt obliged to engage in this oscillating reactive pattern. He believed that this pattern was a cultural phenomenon, not just peculiar to his experience. Coach and coachee reflected how core communicative patterns may be compromising the broader leadership and communication system of the CMC. Significantly, as these patterns were catalyzed within the system, they were becoming ingested within CMC culture. These self-limiting patterns were devaluing work satisfaction, team and individual performance and negatively constructing the 'communication identity' of the CMC, compromising the interface with stakeholder partners, clients and the market and also inhibiting the business from maximizing the potential of its core proposition and brand promise, in the sector it operated within. The following formulation emerged, linking contextual narratives with experience.

Formulation

The *market*: an environment of loss, fear and extreme competition shapes . . .

An organizational *culture* that could be described as 'zero sum game' or a 'win/lose' communicative system – a culture where the only two positions possible are 'winners' and 'losers'; blame is a central dynamic. This dynamic is compounded by . . .

The *relational* style of the chief executives, which was described as 'oppositional' and 'neutralizing', reinforcing the 'win/lose' dynamic; public conflict between them imposes a disturbing leadership effect on team culture and behaviour . . .

The *relational* style of traders and analysts has historically been shaped by this pattern and reinforced it, although there has been some recent success in Bart challenging this relational pattern to a more consensual dynamic . . .

Key individuals, including Bart and the 'difficult' chief executive bring their own patterns of *identity* into the picture where, for different reasons, there are stories of insecurity and lack of confidence. These vulnerabilities contribute to a culture of blame and fear.

In these contexts, individuals within communication *episodes* show a preoccupation with performance but team performance becomes a casualty to an individual 'win' or 'lose' mentality. The system is rife for the emergence of paradoxical patterns, which approximate to the form presented in Figure 6.6 (Cronen *et al.*, 1982; Oliver *et al.*, 2003).

Leadership culture:

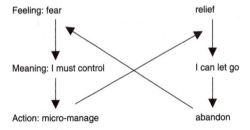

This pattern has ripple effects on team culture, which stimulate stuck defensive behaviour. There is a sense of a lack of forward movement:

Team culture:

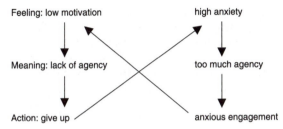

Figure 6.6 **Paradoxical reactive patterns**

Decision

The formulation in Figure 6.6 illustrates paradoxical patterns for both leadership and team culture as a consequence of the contextual influences of culture, relationship and identity and the choices made (interpretive acts) within episodes of communication. Coach and coachee needed to consider whether the coachee could or should exit the pattern, continue the pattern or whether there was a possibility for transformation through reflexive action. In this case, the coachee decided that he would take a courageous step and share his insights with the senior team and invite them to work together on thinking about how to change the dynamic. With regard to his own behaviour, Bart made the decision neither to 'give up' nor to anxiously engage but he began to realize that if he acted with confidence even when there was an environment of instability, the message he gave both his team and his chief executives would be more likely to facilitate a constructive spiral of communication and morale.

Conclusion

This chapter has conceptualized the coaching relationship from a systemic perspective, emphasizing the value of *reflexive agency* for the coachee within their *communication system*. A *reflexive leadership model* has been offered, which links *contextual narratives* to *contextual experiences* and provides possibilities for making sense of these connections and the patterns that emerge from them. It has been proposed that it is useful to think in terms of reactive or reflexive patterns and that the coaching process can facilitate inquiry, reflection and formulation about past, present and future patterns so that the coachee can make an informed decision about his or her action in the leadership *communication system*.

Reflective questions

- Consider an episode of communication within your organization (e.g. university) and hypothesize about the contextual narratives and experiences for yourself and another party.
- What might you hypothesize could be the reflexive choice points within interpretive acts within the episode of communication described?
- In the context of coaching, what do you imagine might be dilemmas for the coach in exercising their own reflexive agency?
- How might you know when there is a paradoxical pattern operating within a communication system?

References

Andersen, T. (1991) *The Reflecting Team: Dialogues and Dialogues about the Dialogues*. New York: Norton.

Barge, K. and Oliver, C. (2003) Working with appreciation in managerial practice. *Academy of Management Review*, 28: 124–142.

Bateson, G. (1972) *Steps to an Ecology of Mind*. Chicago, IL: University of Chicago Press.

Burnham, J. (1986) *Family Therapy*. London: Tavistock.

Campbell, D. (2000) *The Socially Constructed Organization*. London: Karnac.

Cecchin, G., Boscolo, L., Hoffman, L. and Penn, P. (1987) *Milan Systemic Family Therapy*. New York: Basic Books.

Cooperrider, D. and Whitney, D. (2000) A positive revolution in change: appreciative inquiry. In P. Holman and T. Devane (eds) *Collaborating for Change Series*. San Francisco, CA: Berrett-Koehler.

Cronen, V. and Pearce, W.B. (1985) An explanation of how the Milan method works: an invitation to a systemic epistemology and the evolution of family systems. In D. Campbell and R. Draper (eds) *Applications of Systemic Family Therapy: The Milan Approach*. London: Grune and Stratton.

Cronen, V., Johnson, K. and Lannaman, J. (1982) Paradoxes, double binds and reflexive loops: an alternative theoretical perspective. *Family Process*, 21: 91–112.

Dallos, R. and Draper, R. (2005) *Introduction to Family Therapy*. Milton Keynes: Open University Press.

Elkjaer, B. (2001) The learning organization: an undelivered promise. *Management Learning*, 32: 437–452.

Lave, J. and Wenger, E. (1991) *Situated Learning: Legitimate Peripheral Participation*. Cambridge: Cambridge University Press.

Mason, B. (2005) Relational risk taking and the training of supervisors. *Journal of Family Therapy*, 27: 298–301.

Oliver, C. (2005) *Reflexive Inquiry*. London: Karnac.

Oliver Clarke (2010) Website in development.

Oliver, C., Herasymowych, M. and Senko, H. (2003) *Complexity, Relationships and Strange Loops: A Reflexive Practice Guide*. Alberta, Canada: MHA Institute.

Oliver, C., Fitzgerald, S. and Hoxsey, J. (forthcoming, 2010) Appreciative inquiry as a shadow process. *Journal of Management Inquiry*.

O'Neill, M.B. (2007) *Executive Coaching*. San Francisco, CA: John Wiley.

Pearce, W.B. (1989) *Communication and the Human Condition*. Carbondale, IL: Southern Illinois University Press.

Pearce, W.B. (2007) *Making Social Worlds: A Communication Perspective*. Oxford: Blackwell.

Penn, P. (1982) Circular questioning. *Family Process*, 21: 267–280.

Penn, P. (1985) Feed forward: future questions, future maps. *Family Process*, 24: 299–311.

Raelin, J.A. (2001) Public reflection as the basis of learning. *Management Learning*, 32: 11–30.

Tomm, K. (1987) Interventive interviewing part 2: reflexive questioning as a means to enabling self healing. *Family Process*, 26: 167–183.

Van der Haar, D. and Hosking, D.M. (2004) Evaluating appreciative inquiry: a relational constructionist perspective. *Human Relations*, 57: 1017–1036.

Recommended books

Campbell, D. (2000) *The Socially Constructed Organization*. London: Karnac.

Oliver, C. (2005) *Reflexive Inquiry*. London: Karnac.

Oliver, C., Herasymowych, M. and Senko, H. (2003) *Complexity, Relationships and Strange Loops: A Reflexive Practice Guide*. Alberta, Canada: MHA Institute.

Pearce, W.B. (2007) *Making Social Worlds: A Communication Perspective*. Oxford: Blackwell.

7

Coaching across cultures

Lina Daouk-Öyry and Philippe Rosinski

Introduction

Globalisation is changing work as we know it. Many organisations operate worldwide, trade internationally and are composed of increasingly mobile and diverse workers. This means that the coach now typically serves coachees from different cultural backgrounds either within one country (intra-national) or across cultural boundaries (international) (Turner, 2007). As a result, coaches and in particular work or executive coaches are increasingly facing a new challenge in their practice, which is the influence of culture (St Claire-Ostwald, 2007). Whether working for multi-national clients or with a multicultural workforce within one country, the coach's role is now likely to comprise the following aspects:

- understanding various cultural preferences and their implications for coaching, which includes the coach's own 'cultural lens' as well as the coachees';
- dealing constructively with cultural differences, which may manifest themselves in potential bias and stereotyping, and helping our coachees do the same;
- appreciating that behaviour is a product of our environment (culture) and own natural preferences (personality);
- acknowledging that culture is a fluid and transient concept that goes beyond national cultures and ethnic origin.

Culture in everyday language is used to refer to the national origin of people. However, this is not the only group they can belong to. Each individual can be influenced by several cultures at any one time, all of which impact on behaviour. We will begin this chapter by defining culture and coaching from a multi-national perspective. While illustrating with examples and case studies, we will then explore the ways in which individuals can differ through the Cultural Orientations Framework (COF™) (Rosinski, 2003). We will conclude this chapter with key learning points raised.

Coaching in multi-national contexts

The national origin of coachees is not synonymous with culture or at least it is not the only 'culture' that influences behaviour. Interpreting culture as a feature that is only derived from national origin (e.g. Chinese, Italian, Hungarian) limits the influence of culture to a narrow spectrum. While we will focus on the national aspect to some extent, we highlight that culture is a multifaceted concept.

Rosinski (2003: 20) explains that a 'group's culture is a set of unique characteristics that distinguish its members from another group'. A 'group' could be a nation, an organisation, a society, a gender, an age or any other group distinguishable from others (Rosinski, 2003). Therefore, it is not only nations that have their own 'unique set of characteristics' or 'culture', but also other groups such as women, older people, political groups and so on. In other words, culture refers to the 'humanmade' aspects of individuals' environment or to the influence of 'nurture'.

Thus, different cultures can exert simultaneous influences on individual identity (Rosinski, 2003: 21). For example, a person can be German, a student, female and an atheist simultaneously. Each of these roles represents a culture and the stronger the culture of the group, the more likely it is to predominate in shaping behaviour and forming identity (Peterson, 2007). To illustrate, a strong organisational culture can lead employees to exhibit behaviours (goal orientation, people orientation etc.) that are congruent with the culture of their organisation rather than their national background. For example, Hofstede's (2003) research on a sample of countries from the Arab world revealed that individuals working in this part of the world have a strong tendency for avoiding uncertainty. In an organisational setting, this may result in an organisational culture that embraces and encourages the implementation of strict rules and regulations to ensure minimisation of uncertainty. This organisational culture may then be so strong that it affects the orientation of, say, Malaysian employees working in any Arab firms, even though their national orientation is directed towards accepting uncertainty (Hofstede, 2003). Hofstede's seminal contribution to the literature involves a rather static and categorising approach to culture. Rosinski's dynamic and inclusive view of culture, by contrast, has a different application, which is global coaching.

The complexity of the concept of culture and its effect on the individual's behaviour renders *understanding cultural differences* essential to the coaching process. However, this can sometimes lead to falling into the trap of stereotyping (Peterson, 2007). That is, a good understanding of the coachee's *national culture* might lead to wrongly assuming that they will typically exhibit certain behaviours associated with that culture. This is not always true because of the effect of *other* cultures as well as personality on behaviour. A study by Rojon (2007) assessing the cultural orientation of professionals in the UK and Germany using the COF™ revealed that differences between men and women with regards to cultural orientation were bigger than differences between UK and German respondents. Another example is that the cultural gap between a young Japanese girl and her grandparents could be greater than any differences between her and a young French girl. In this case, the influences of the peer group might be stronger than the influence of national origin, which might make for not necessarily stereotypical Japanese but rather typically female teenage behaviours.

We also need to understand that behaviour is not only influenced by nurture, different cultures, but also nature, our own individual preferences, which psychologists refer to as 'personality'. Cross-cultural research, which makes comparisons across nations, has shown that for instance the most widely accepted model of personality, the 'Big Five', is very similar across some countries but by no means all (Costa and McCrae, 1992; Cheung *et al.*, 2001).

Therefore, key to understanding cultural differences is to understand that while people come from different cultural backgrounds, they can be similar in many ways, such as how organised or punctual they are, even when these character-istics are not typical of their national culture (Peterson, 2007). Conversely, individuals from the same national cul-ture could be different in many respects, such as personality, gender, age and so on.

Cultural differences are encountered during the coach-ing process either intra-nationally or inter-nationally. In intra-national settings, the coach deals with a multicultural workforce within one country, whereas in inter-national set-tings the coach deals with coachees across national bound-aries in addition to other cultural differences (Peterson, 2007; Turner, 2007).

Example: the UK and Sweden

Consider this example of inter-cultural challenges taken from Rosinski (2003). This concerns two geographically close countries, where the coachee, Will, is a British director of the UK operations of an international company who is assigned to manage the Nordic office where most of the employees are Swedish. Will takes offence at seeing his Swedish colleagues' perceived lack of commitment, as he interprets it, when the pressure of business is on. Rosinski (2003) argues that being 'calm in face of adversity' is a qual-ity cherished in Sweden and considered as a positive skill. However, Will perceives the calmness of the Swedish employees as a lack of commitment. He fails to understand that individuals perceive the world from different view-points. This causes friction in the team, as he is perceived as 'stuck up' and 'obsessed with punctuality and detail'. Will's boss encourages him to work with a coach versed in dealing with international clients to help him appreciate different viewpoints and approaches to work and to look in new direc-tions for interpretations and solutions.

Case study: 'Marie'

Marie, the business developer for Asia of a prestigious, global, consumer-service company with headquarters in the UK, asks for your help. Marie's boss suggested that she work with a coach, which is unusual; her company seldom invests much in ongoing training for its people. Marie is thus surprised, and feels privileged to benefit from a coaching programme. You were highly recommended to her, but live in Europe; Marie, a US citizen of Anglo-Saxon descent, asks you if you can coach her in Beijing, where she has lived for the last year.

Marie tells you that she wants to use the coaching to become more effective in developing the business in the region. In a few years, she wants to have established the Asian region as one of the main business centres for her company. She also mentions that she is constantly working, and can never relax enough to simply be; she always has to be doing something: work, reading or study. She wants to share more time with her husband.

With Marie's approval, you talk with her functional and regional bosses (she reports equally to both in a matrix format) to determine what they expect from a coaching programme. Through these two direct supervisors, you are informed of the following: Marie's regional boss, Joe, a British citizen living in Beijing, describes Marie as an outstanding professional with an incredible workload capacity, dealing with multiple, complex situations. 'Marie', he says, 'is devoted to the success of the business and obtains outstanding results. She has been sent to difficult, emerging markets in Eastern Europe to troubleshoot problems and has been able to get projects through, resolved, and in a timely manner. Socially, she is charming and pleasant, but at work she is very pushy when promoting her ideas. When she delegates, she relentlessly comes back to her direct reports to see what has been accomplished.' Joe reports that this, too, is perceived as pushy.

Joe continues, 'Her Asian teams, from Japan, India, and Beijing, tend to shy away from working directly with her. She has been known to shout at her direct reports publicly and humiliate other colleagues in front of their bosses. Even clients have been subject to her wrath', Joe whispers. 'She needs to create a team spirit and have people happy to work with her.'

Joe pauses to think and then continues, 'After an argument, Marie might try to make amends with the person she has upset, but she cannot stop herself from competing to win the argument, even if it will cost her the relationship. Many of her colleagues think she has a need to compete and have the last word.'

'What has surprised more than one of her colleagues is that Marie's self-confidence at work contrasts noticeably with her submissive attitude with her (functional) boss, Jane.' Joe then pauses, and continues, 'I have noticed that she walks briskly into the office. She looks tense. When she is annoyed with a discussion, she rolls her eyes and walks away.'

Marie's functional boss, Jane, an American based in the US, summarises Marie's attitude as, 'She lacks confidence. Marie remains silent in meetings.' She continues, 'She wants to impress people and overcompensates. She tries to impress people that she is bright, and what would we do without her. When she encounters resistance with her direct reports, she becomes aggressive, hierarchical, very top-down. She has little to no empathy or social radar. She is perceived as having little sensitivity to what is required by others.' Jane pauses and says thoughtfully, 'She does not know how to profile herself to engage people.'

Marie tells you that she is 42 years old, has been married for 12 years, and has no children. She was raised in the eastern US, and comes from a traditional, middle-class family. Her husband is a very successful Swiss banker, who has been promoted every few years and changed countries with each promotion. Marie says that she has usually found a way to follow him while pursuing her career or studies. She also mentions that her husband admires her achievements but complains sometimes that she relies too much on him to make decisions.

When Marie gives some information on her background, you find out that she has an older brother who was the apple of their parents' eyes. All hopes were focused on his career, until he decided to quit the business life to live in a retreat. She was an average student at school, but once her brother left the business world, Marie began to have outstanding results at school.

Marie talks proudly about the results she has achieved and her constant travels. She confides in you that she is driven by her own agenda and gets upset when anything gets in her way. She knows that she is perceived as pushy, and she wants to learn how to inspire rather than impose. Her company has given her the opportunity to receive coaching to work on developing her emotional intelligence, which she understands as developing her interpersonal skills. With this background information from Marie and her two bosses, your assessment of the coaching situation begins.

(Burrus, 2006)

Reflective questions:

- What are the potential cultural factors, such as dominant cultural orientations for any of the parties involved?
- What else may be at play here?
- How might you approach coaching Marie?

Whether the coach is working inter- or intra-nationally, sensitivity to cultural differences is a recursive process. While the coach needs to ensure a good understanding of these dynamics in order to disseminate them, coachees also bring new perspectives and experiences that can expand the coach's perspective. For example, in a coaching session with an Egyptian coachee who was engaged in the process but who kept on answering his telephone during the meeting, Rosinski was initially surprised and slightly uncomfortable with this behaviour. But Rosinski appreciated being able to reach another Mediterranean professional whenever he needed to, which made him realise that this meant that he was probably interrupting other meetings in order to do that. Similarly, people from other nationalities resident in the UK have observed that British people are usually very polite in direct interactions, making it difficult to understand when they are not happy. That is, having no feedback or good feedback from a British client does not always mean that things are good, as it could be merely a reflection of their politeness. The coach might have to use different ways for getting the information they require from the coachee.

Cross-cultural challenges in coaching

Coaching is a cross-disciplinary profession that attracts individuals from different professional backgrounds such as consultants, executives and managers, perhaps less so psychologists and counsellors (Grant and Zackon, 2004). Rosinski (2003) suggests that there should be a move from traditional coaching where objectives are personal and corporate to a more global view of coaching where objectives, although personal, can reap benefits that extend beyond the coachee and the organisation. While traditional executive coaching mainly focuses on two fundamental perspectives (psychological and managerial) (Rosinski, 2003), global coaching expands beyond traditional coaching to tap into multiple perspectives such as cultural, spiritual, physical and so on (Rosinski, 2006). Global coaches help coachees and ultimately their clients to expand their worldview and look in new directions for solutions (Abbott and Rosinski, 2007), where we refer you back to our examples above. For instance, consider Marie. What might the multiple issues be for her, not only in her professional life but also her personal life? How can the coach extend his/her worldview to embrace the complexity and interconnectivity that characterises today's context?

We refer the reader to Rosinski's article 'Coaching from multiple perspectives' (Rosinski, 2006) for more detailed discussion, but let us at least share some elements here. Tackling the professional issues first, Marie's aims are to establish the business in Asia, yet her Asian colleagues are shying away from working directly with her. The coach could usefully employ the political perspective here in order to help her deal with this particular aspect. 'Politics is an activity that builds and maintains your power so that you can achieve your goals' (Rosinski, 1998: 1). Marie has been winning arguments at the cost of estranging herself from others in the organisation. The approach that she is adopting is weakening her relationship with potential allies who could be supporting her in developing the business in the region. These behavioural strategies may also be linked to her personal preference, for instance it is feasible that if given a 'Big Five' personality assessment she would score low on agreeableness. It takes a curious coach, open to the complex reality, to navigate through these multiple possible origins of behaviour and to foster progress.

Taking another perspective in this case study (physical), Marie has been keeping herself so busy with work, reading and studying that she does not have enough time to relax. This is in line with a very protestant work ethic, which is prevalent in Anglo-Saxon countries, but might also link to personal preferences, where one way of dealing with stress is simply not to stop. This work–life imbalance has consequences on her stress levels and can have further consequences on her physical health in general. The global coach could help Marie set specific targets to promote her well-being, reduce her stress levels and develop resilience (Rosinski, 2006).

A framework for understanding culture – the COF™ categories

There are many potential dimensions that culturally diverse individuals differ on and that influence the dynamics of coaching. We base our discussion on the model on which Rosinski's (2003) Cultural Orientations Framework (COF™) is based as (a) it was developed based on the work of several interculturalists, anthropologists, and others such as Kluckhohn and Stodtbeck, Hall, Trompenaars, and Hofstede, which makes it comprehensive, and (b) it encompasses dimensions that are directly relevant to coaching. The dimensions are bipolar, and individuals or cultures could lie anywhere on the continuum that links these two sides. The position of individuals in a given context on this continuum could be referred to as *cultural orientation*, which is 'the inclination to think, feel, or act in a way that is culturally determined' (Rosinski, 2003: 51). Conversely, the cultural orientation towards one pole does not imply that the individual will not exhibit behaviours associated with the opposite pole. For example, individuals culturally habitually orientated towards 'direct communication' might exhibit 'indirect communication' in certain situations such as in formal meetings or when meeting people for the first time.

Several important nuances distinguish the COF™ from previous models. Among these nuances are:

- **Merit**. The choice of words should convey the potential merit of each orientation. For example, Rosinski chose the term *humility* instead of *subjugation to nature* coined by Kluckhohn and Stodtbeck (1961).
- **Essence**. Rosinski has clung closely to the essence of dimensions, which lie in the etymology. For example, he has defined *monochronic time* simply as 'concentrate on one activity and/or relationship at a time' in contrast to *polychronic time* ('concentrate simultaneously on multiple tasks and/or relationships') (Rosinski, 2003: 96). Hall's (1976) original concept includes other notions such as scheduling and compartmentalisation, which do not necessarily relate to the duality monochronic/polychronic time *per se*.
- **Dialectics**. Most importantly, Rosinski is less interested in describing static and binary traits of a culture (e.g. the French are like this, the Americans are like that) than in having a vocabulary to depict dynamic and complex cultural features. Aristotle declared that 'out of two contradictory propositions, if one is true, the other must be false'. Ironically, this is true and false at the same time! *Binary thinking* (*or*) tends to promote polarisation and division. *Dialectics* (*and*) is called for to find new ways to reconcile alternatives, leverage differences and enable unity in diversity (Rosinski, 2003: 57–58).

The COF™ model proposes seven main categories that expand into 17 dimensions or culture orientations, represented in Table 7.1.

Table 7.1 COF™ categories and dimensions

COF™ categories	Dimensions
1 Sense of power and responsibility	Control/Harmony/Humility
2 Time management approaches	Scarce/Plentiful Monochronic/Polychronic Past/Present/Future
3 Identity and purpose	Being/Doing Individualistic/Collectivistic
4 Organisational arrangements	Hierarchy/Equality Universalist/Particularist Stability/Change Competitive/Collaborative
5 Territory	Protective/Sharing
6 Communication patterns	High context/Low context Direct/Indirect Affective Neutral Formal/Informal
7 Modes of thinking	Deductive/Inductive Analytical/Systemic

1 Our sense of power and responsibility

There are three ways in which we can relate to the world in general, and more specifically to our businesses and our own careers: (a) we can seek to control; (b) we can be humble where we accept natural limitations; (c) we can also strive for harmony and balance with nature.

We encourage our coachees to work with each of these. They can take responsibility for their lives, follow their dreams, and strive for excellence and advancement – a stance of control that can provide motivation and lead to positive self-fulfilling prophecies. At the same time, they can accept natural limitations of both themselves and their situations. Knowing one's limits is not always obvious, but humbly accepting them is paradoxically within one's control. Harmony is about acting with determination as much as necessary, and letting go as much as possible.

2 *The way we manage time*

There are different cultural orientations to managing time. For example, many executives see time as a *scarce* resource. An alternative orientation is to view time as *plentiful*. For the coachee who sees time as scarce and gets caught in a daily flurry of activities without meaningful actions, we might discuss strategies for opening up opportunities for reflective thought – while at the same time making use of their capacity for high-speed action. By viewing time in a plentiful fashion, the coachee may paradoxically appreciate the scarcity of time.

3 *How we define our identity and purpose*

In defining identity and purpose, it is common for executives to refer to how much they do and achieve – a *doing* orientation. Another orientation is to stress living itself and the development of talents and relationships – a *being* orientation. For example, with coachees whose preferences are for doing a lot at the expense of productive and meaningful relationships in the workplace, we may encourage them to try new strategies for building trusting, sustainable relationships. Not only can they then do more, but they may also receive the benefits of a richer personal and professional life.

4 *The organisational arrangements we favour*

One way in which people differ on organisational arrangements is in the degree to which they are *competitive* or *collaborative*. In competitive cultures, the workplace is often the stage for a contest between individuals or work areas. The aim is to win. In collaborative cultures, the emphasis is more on working together. The European Union is an example of leveraging competition and collaboration. Countries strive to be the best. Governments regularly compare their performance with their neighbours' to motivate performance – but there is also collaboration. Best practices are exchanged in all areas: science, engineering medicine and so on.

5 *Our notions of territory and boundaries*

In *protective* cultures, people are keen to protect their physical and mental territory. They like to keep their physical and psychological distance. In *sharing* cultures, people seek closeness and intimacy and in the workplace they freely discuss personal subjects as well as business matters. Coachees who favour a protective approach can be encouraged towards a sharing orientation through greater self-disclosure. This can promote greater protection through establishing a network of relationships built on trust. The stronger network also builds productivity benefits.

6 *The way we communicate*

There are many variations across cultures in how people communicate. For example, US business practice is typified by a *direct* communication style where the priority is to get one's point across. In many Asian cultures, an *indirect* style is favoured, where the priority is to maintain a cordial relationship. To leverage the two orientations, we suggest being clear and firm with the content while being careful and sensitive with the form. Some coaches hold bluntness as a virtue and will challenge coachees directly as a sign of courage and honesty. This approach may well backfire across cultures. By holding to the substance but being sensitive with regard to the process, coaches can leverage difference for the benefit of the coachee.

7 *Our modes of thinking*

Much recent research has proven that there is a large variation between cultures on modes of thinking. For example, some cultures tend to favour *analytical thinking*. Analysis breaks a whole into parts and problems are solved through decomposition. In other cultures, *systemic thinking* is more common. Systemic or 'holistic' thinking brings the parts together into a cohesive whole. Emphasis is on connections between the parts and on the entire system. A synthesis is needed as Blaise Pascal (Rosinski, 2003: 187) already argued in the seventeenth century when he declared: 'I consider [it] impossible to know the parts without knowing the whole, and to know the whole without particularly knowing the parts'.

The COF™ online assessment has been developed by Rosinski to help individuals, teams and organisations use the model as an assessment tool. We invite the reader to find out more about the tool and to try it out at www.philrosinski.com/cof

---

Case study: Using COF™ assessment in team coaching

This case study presents some of the COF™ aggregate results of a group of 58 coachees; 54 of whom are from the UK, two are from France, one is from Denmark and one is from Germany. This is not a group of employees working within one team *per se*; the results should nevertheless reflect the type of information the COF™ produces and how it can be used within a team. For this purpose, we will focus only on select dimensions and examples of questions a coach might use with such a group.

When using COF™ with teams, the coach should consider what dimensions are overused or overlooked. A close investigation on such phenomena in this case study revealed that the dominant orientation in the *stability/change* dimension was *change*, with 85% of the group favouring working in hectic environments that promote adaptability and innovation. On the positive side, coaches promote change in their work but change is not always the solution. With a limited inclination and self-evaluated ability for stability, the question is: What are the merits of stability that you might overlook? In coaching, the ideal combination often includes alternating between periods of change and periods of stability. Being in constant change could become counterproductive and the important question to ask is: Are these individuals taking enough time to recuperate and consolidate what they have? For this group, the danger would be to strive for new and radical changes at times when consolidation, disciplined maintenance and systematic improvement of existing processes would be necessary.

As another example, this group showed an orientation towards *control*, with 73% claiming a good to excellent ability to take responsibility. This is undeniably an important asset in setting and achieving targets. However, only 2% showed an orientation towards *humility*. This orientation can indeed be ineffective when it leads to a passive acceptance of fate and to preventing the coachee from positive change. However, humility can also be very helpful because it is important to understand that things can be out of control sometimes and this will relieve some of the burden of always feeling responsible for what happens (Rosinski, 2003). This group should be encouraged to think about the advantages of a control orientation in order to consolidate them. But they should also be invited to think about the situations where this orientation is not helpful and the risk associated with the temptation to succeed whatever it takes. Learning to accept natural limitations and leveraging humility with control is a good opportunity for development for this group.

Interestingly, these results were very similar to ones from another group of executives from a multi-national company. Perhaps the similarity in the change/stability dimension could be attributed to the fact that this team was working in a company that encourages innovation. However, the control/humility similarity could potentially be the reflection of a western cultural orientation.

Dealing with cultural differences

Culture can stand as a barrier in the face of the coaching process if it is not understood and dealt with effectively. The good news is that culture can also become an opportunity. The coach needs to understand cultural differences and work on shifting their own and their coachees' perspectives to open new routes for achieving meaningful, important objectives. Understanding cultural differences and dealing with them productively is a stepwise process that demands both open-mindedness and perseverance. It also requires the recognition that culture is fluid, changing and situational but nevertheless intertwined with natural and more stable individual preferences. Rosinski (2003) adapted Bennett's (1993) six-stage model to provide a framework for developing intercultural sensitivity in coaching. The model outlines the steps during the advancement towards understanding and dealing with cultural differences. While the model applies to all parties in coaching, it is crucial for coaches to advance through the steps themselves before assisting the coachees in doing so. The route to understanding cultural differences starts from not acknowledging their existence, then progressively recognising them until one can leverage them. The ethnocentric attitude can take three forms:

- ignoring differences;
- recognising differences but evaluating them negatively;
- recognising differences but minimising their importance.

Coaching across cultures involves instead:

- recognising and accepting differences;
- adapting to differences;
- integrating differences;
- leveraging differences.

The further people progress onto further steps, the more effective they become in dealing with differences. Leveraging differences is the highest level of intercultural sensitivity that individuals can reach; it assumes that individuals can critically think about culture, treasure what they value in their culture, adopt what they believe is valuable from other culture(s) and synthesise the differences. Individuals who can leverage cultural differences would benefit the most from interactions with other cultures through capitalising on their understanding of their own culture while learning from other cultures.

Conclusion

Traditional executive coaching has assumed a worldview that is not universal and may prove increasingly insufficient in addressing the complex challenges in our turbulent, interconnected and global environment. It is time to weave the richness of cultural diversity into coaching, embrace diversity, bridge cultural gaps, learn from cultural differences and release higher potential in individuals. This will enable greater and sustainable success by making the most of alternative cultural perspectives to the benefit of people, organisations and the world at large.

Reflective questions

- What are your cultural orientations?
- How do these orientations possibly vary depending on the context?
- How do your cultural orientations impact the way you coach/lead?
- What are the orientations of people you coach and the key differences with yours?
- How do you reconcile the differences?
- How are you learning and growing from this, enriching your own cultures, expanding your options when coaching/ leading and living?

References

Abbott, G. and Rosinski, P. (2007) Global coaching and evidence based coaching: multiple perspectives operating in a process of pragmatic humanism. *International Journal of Evidence Based Coaching and Mentoring*, 5: 58–77.

Bennett, M. (1993) Towards ethnorelativism: a developmental model of intercultural sensitivity. In R.M. Paige (ed.) *Education for the Intercultural Experience* (pp. 21–71). Yarmouth, ME: Intercultural Press.

Burrus, K. (2006) Marie's case study. Workshop 'Leveraging multiple perspectives: practicing on a concrete and complex case', co-facilitated with Philippe Rosinski and presented at the International Coach Federation European Conference, Brussels, Belgium, May.

Cheung, F.M., Leung, K., Zhang, J.X., Sun, H.F., Gan, Y.Q., Song, W.Z. and Xie, D. (2001) Indigenous Chinese personality construct:

is the Five Factor Model complete? *Journal of Cross-Cultural Psychology*, 32: 407–433.

Costa, P.T., Jr and McCrae, R.R. (1992) *The Revised NEO Personality Inventory and NEO Five Factor Inventory: Professional Manual*. Odessa, FL: Psychological Assessment Resources.

Grant, A.M. and Zackon, R. (2004) Executive, workplace and life coaching: findings from a large scale survey of international coach federation members. *International Journal of Evidenced-Based Coaching and Mentoring*, 2: 1–15.

Hall, E. (1976) *Beyond Culture*. New York: Doubleday.

Hofstede, G. (2003) Geert Hofstede cultural dimensions. Retrieved August 2008, from www.geert-hofstede.com

Kluckhohn, F.R. and Strodtbeck, F.L. (1961) *Variations in Values Orientations*. Evanston, IL: Row, Peterson.

Peterson, D.B. (2007) Executive coaching in a cross-cultural context. *Consulting Psychology Journal: Practice and Research*, 59: 261–271.

Rojon, C. (2007) Culture, personality and competency: assessing individual behavioural styles, a cross-cultural validation study of the Cultural Orientations Framework (COF™) assessment questionnaire. Unpublished MSc dissertation, University of Surrey, London.

Rosinski, P. (1998) Constructive politics: essential for leadership. *Leadership in Action*, 18: 1–5.

Rosinski, P. (2003) *Coaching across Cultures*. London: Nicholas Brealey Publishing.

Rosinski, P. (2006) Coaching from multiple perspectives. *International Journal of Coaching in Organizations*, 4: 16–23.

St Claire-Ostwald, B. (2007) Carrying cultural baggage: the contribution of socio-cultural anthropology to cross-cultural coaching. *International Journal of Evidence Based Coaching and Mentoring*, 5: 45–52.

Turner, R.A. (2007) Coaching and consulting in multi-cultural contexts. *Consulting Psychology Journal: Practice and Research*, 59: 241–243.

Recommended book

Rosinski, P. (2003) *Coaching across Cultures*. London: Nicholas Brealey Publishing.

8

The issue of power in the coaching relationship

Peter Welman and Tatiana Bachkirova

Introduction

A coach strongly believes in the value of his toolkit for reaching the goal of the coaching session and imposes on the coachee one exercise after another without any clarity as to their aims.

The coachee asks the coach to push him to the limit in order to achieve what he wants to achieve. The coach takes on this role and coaches in an unusually forceful manner. Neither party is comfortable with the process; however, the coachee is satisfied with the outcome.

What is the single dynamic at issue in both these cases? Sampson (1985: 125, 126) argues that it is the will to exercise power – that single urge, in both men and women, to impose our will on our fellow being. Whether in the home, the office, the street or the coaching room, the *nature* of imposition remains the same. The degree may vary, but 'dominato' itself, as Sampson writes, is always 'dominato'. This 'will' has a long history, some might say as long as history itself. Hobbes (1651: 47), for example, wrote of a 'restless desire' of 'all mankind' for 'power after power that ceaseth only in death'. He also, more mildly, called it the 'general inclination' of us all. Whether it is, in fact, a 'restless desire' or a 'general inclination' and whether it is 'of us all' is perhaps something we can only answer for ourselves, but the evidence of recorded history and the pre-occupations of our time would suggest, at the very least, that it is a key dimension of human existence.

It is also widely accepted that power affects relationships. And so it is perhaps surprising, given that the quality of the relationship between the helper and the client is proven to be crucial (Clarkson, 2000; Kilburg, 2004; O'Broin and Palmer, 2007; Wampold, 2001), that the topic of power has been largely ignored in the coaching literature. This chapter is an attempt to help redress this balance and to make clear some of the issues with which the coach is likely to contend.

In drawing these ideas together we have tried to keep uppermost in mind what might be most useful to the coach. At times this emphasis sits uncomfortably with philosophical exactness, but, in a field where there is so little agreement as to nature and form, this is perhaps inevitable. It is also our view that, ultimately, language is the approximation, while the *experience of power* itself is usually all too real.

The purpose of this chapter, then, is to increase the awareness of the coach of some of the issues that power presents in the coaching relationship. First, we identify the form of power that we think is an issue and compare it with related concepts. Then we explore why coaches need to pay attention to this phenomenon, illustrating our points within three specific dimensions of the coaching relationship. The chapter concludes with recommendations for coaches.

Defining power in relationship

Little agreement exists as to an exact definition of 'power'. Philosophers and other social scientists find themselves disagreeing as to what it is, who has it and when, whether it is a good thing or not, whether we should aspire to have more of it or less, and so on (Fromm, 1960; Lukes, 1987; Kipnis, 2001). However, for our purposes, we wish to identify two well-accepted meanings:

- one is *power over somebody*, the ability to dominate him or her, to impose one's will on them; and

- the other is *power to do something*, to be able to, to be potent.

Both these definitions sit at the very heart of the coaching endeavour – the former as a perpetual potential and the latter as, arguably, the essence of coaching itself. Coaching is often described as *empowering* people to reach their potential, to develop new skills and to be able to use them effectively, while its associated term 'powerlessness' is used to describe a state of *not* being able to do what one wants. Furthermore, these twin meanings of power may actually appear *together*, for example when a coach explores the relationship between a coachee (seeking potency) and their employing organisation (experienced as 'impositional'). In both these cases academics and practitioners may find themselves using a single term to describe impulses that could hardly be more distinct. They may also find themselves slipping from one definition to the other without noticing, obscuring the analysis and perhaps avoiding the issue.

That these terms are not only central and contrasting but are furthermore antithetical should also not escape our notice. Fromm (1960: 140), for example, suggests that a person with a lack of potency is more likely to strive for domination: 'the extent to which an individual is potent, that is, able to realise his potentialities on the basis of freedom and integrity of his self, he does not need to dominate and is lacking the lust for power'. If he is right, it would appear that these particular 'twins' are neither identical nor compatible.

Another useful distinction is of that between power (as imposition) and influence. Clearly we are influencing each other all the time – for how else would we get our needs met? – and yet this form of social exchange does not, *in itself*, involve imposition. The exact point where influence becomes imposition is difficult to identify in absolute analytical terms in *all* relationships, including coaching and counselling. Consider, for example, the account of Milton Erickson's intervention with a deeply depressed lady who lived in Milwaukee (Erikson, in Zeig, 1980). Having seen flourishing African violets and an open Bible in her home, he 'prescribed' that she give as a gift to members of her church (for clearly she was a church-goer, he concluded) an African violet on all appropriate occasions (births, marriages, christenings, etc.). If she did that she would be well, he assured her, and left. Years later he heard of the death of 'The African Violet Queen of Milwaukee'. 'Anybody who takes care of that many African violets is too busy to be depressed,' he said. 'I only saw her once' (Zeig, 1980: 828).

At first sight his actions might be considered bordering on imposition, and yet we do not know if there was actual imposition of one person's will on another. Certainly, he was influential, perhaps charismatic. Maybe the lady was daunted by his reputation. None of these things we know for sure. Ultimately what actually happened is an experiential issue rather than an analytically verifiable one. We would need to enquire into his motivations and her reactions to determine the particular case, as we will discuss later in the chapter in relation to coaching.

Why investigate power?

However compelling may be the use of power as potency, we choose to explore here the meaning of power as domination. As this book is about relationship we need to address the issues that the urge to personal ascendancy may bring. It may sound extreme to be considering it for a profession grounded on libertarian principles and yet it is well known that counselling and psychotherapy, based on equally laudable aims and objectives, and more professionally regulated, has a history of cases and debates about precisely this topic (Masson, 1989; Spinnelli, 1994; Clarkson, 2000). There is also a growing body of literature concerning power in the mentoring relationship (Ragins, 1997; Schmidt, 1997; Klasen and Clutterbuck, 2002; Manathunga, 2007). It is clearly an issue that warrants attention.

As we approach this subject there is little doubt in our minds that we are entering emotionally turbulent waters. The definition of power as imposition is almost guaranteed to raise emotional reactions in the perpetrator *and* in the recipient of their actions (Sampson, 1965, 1985). And yet it is precisely this *emotional turbulence* that makes the topic so important. There is, for example, research that suggests that, when emotionally aroused, the neurological pathways to the higher cortex (the thinking brain) are impeded, and, in extreme circumstances, cut off, so that the emotional brain can attend (without questioning thought) to our immediate survival needs (Griffin and Tyrrell, 2003). To exert power over someone or to have someone's will imposed on us, *is* emotionally arousing. It follows, therefore, that to the extent that we are engaged in these emotionally arousing matters we will not be at our rational best, and neither will our coachee. Hawkins and Smith (2006: 293) provide a vivid example of this happening to an experienced coach when he was 'inexplicably' intimidated by a coachee: 'I began burbling about what I did, and felt almost in my "panic zone" ... All my experience and skill ... deserted me'.

There is a further reason for looking at this issue in these terms. When coaches sense where the line between influence and imposition falls, it may free them to explore with more creativity areas of legitimate influence that they may not yet have ventured to use. One of the features of the coaching relationship is the extent to which the coach should 'push' the coachee. There is some evidence to suggest that the coach may be over-protective of the boundaries of the process while their coachee, more concerned with outcome, would like them to be bolder (Hawkins and Smith, 2006; Gyllensten and Palmer, 2007). Knowing where the line falls grants the coach more freedom of legitimate movement, with potential benefit to their coachee.

Finally, there is a more homely reason for our enquiry into this side of coaching. The teenage son of one of us recently said that he was exploring the dark side of music and films and, when asked about his motivation, replied that he had had a happy childhood and now wanted to see the shadows. With a psychologist's hat on, one might say he felt sufficiently safe and secure to explore the darker sides of life. In similar vein, we feel sufficiently confident about the coaching endeavour to explore the shady edges, if they be there, and in so doing enhance our understanding of the territory. Staying with the wisdom of youth, we might contend with Christopher Robin that, if we know where the lines are, the bears may not get us (Milne, 2004).

The nature of power as imposition

The nature of imposition is often elusive and subtle. To own the desire to impose one's will on another person is not the easiest acknowledgement for any of us. As much of the literature suggests, it does not exactly put us in a good light (Fromm, 1960; Sampson, 1985; McClelland, 1987; Greene, 2006). In fact we may even have well-rehearsed explanations of how we are working to avoid doing just this, and indeed why we are working as coaches at all – to help others resist the imposition of those around them, for example. But the matter is more elusive than that. For one thing, the urge to excel may be subconscious; we may even not be aware of how, or indeed *that*, we are doing it.

Second, there are elements of 'perception' and 'reception' to be considered. What is *considered* an 'imposition' may vary between people, circumstances and contexts. There are no guarantees that our best (or worst) intentions will be interpreted as such by the recipient of our behaviour (Bargh and Alvarez, 2001). If we are looking to define what is 'real' on any occasion we need to look beyond the intentions of the perpetrator. It may also be argued that there are dimensions of power embedded in the context that we may have become so used to working within that we lose sight of them as bindings at all. If periodically they begin to chafe, we may even put them down as inevitable – part of the natural order.

Third, power, as imposition, is not only an important aspect of relationship, it *requires* a relationship. You cannot exert power on your own; you need someone to exert it *over*. Some authors have gone so far as to say that relationships themselves are 'power in flux' (Spinelli, 1994), as if you cannot avoid being in a relationship of power by virtue of being 'in relationship'. This determinism is also evident in some of the sociological literature. We see these definitions as suffering from a single fallacy, namely that while the potential for power may be ubiquitous – part of the fabric of life – the *(f)act* of power (being *exerted* at any one time) is *never* inevitable. And it is by making 'power as imposition' explicit that we are able both to focus on the possibility of 'benign' relationships giving rise to acts of imposition *and* to avoid the limitations of structural determinism (Masson, 1989; Ragins, 1997). We agree with Spinelli's (1994) criticism of Masson (1989) that just because it is possible does not mean that it will be manifest. It is the language of 'pre-disposition to' and 'possibility of' power which we find more helpful in the coaching context.

It is with these thoughts in mind that we turn our attention to specific dimensions of the coaching relationship. The following are three groups of factors that coaches may find useful to consider:

- factors influencing the predisposition to exercise power in the coach;
- contextual issues, including the power of the coachee;
- dealing with power in the immediacy of the coaching interaction.

Factors influencing the predisposition to exercise power in the coach

Coaches are sometimes commissioned to work with coachees more successful than they were themselves in their previous careers. This may give rise within the coach to feelings of insecurity and inadequacy. As a way of compensating for this situation they may seek to dominate, for example, by holding on disproportionately to the process itself, denying the coachee their fair share of control.

Fear of the unpredictability of the coaching process is often a reason for imposing unnecessary structure on the session, with the overuse of models and techniques. This reason for domination is most often reported by less experienced coaches who may seek to demonstrate credibility by the application of a forceful pace to the session and by the extensive use of structured activities. One of the consequences of this may be that the coach comes to view the coachee as no longer being the primary agent of their own behaviour. They may even come to value their tools as more instrumental than the coachee's own resources and effort. There is evidence to suggest, for example, that cognitive-behavioural therapists, who are known for their extensive use of tools, may be less likely than others to attribute gains in therapy to their clients' own efforts and motivation (Zimbardo, 1970; Mitchell *et al.*, 1977; Kipnis, 1984, 2001). Kipnis offers the above as an explanation of why we may come to *devalue* those whom we are most able to control.

Another temptation to exercise power may stem from the attachment of coaches to specific outcomes of the coaching process. If they are overly concerned with their reputation as coaches, for example, they may be tempted to exert unnecessary pressure on the coachee in order to demonstrate a tangible outcome of coaching. And even if they are not so tempted, *any* attachment to outcome runs the risk of *conceding* power to others, which may equally distort the process.

Among the *means* that are available to coaches if they wish to exercise power, is their *status* as specialists who are in a position to deliver a service that is needed by the organisation or an individual coachee. In spite of some voices that still argue against the professionalisation of coaching, this process is under way and coaches enjoy their status, particularly when their services have been sought out.

The professional status of coaches is closely linked to the image of an expert in a particular field. The myth of professional *expertise* as a symbol of power has already been explored in other professions (Illich, 1971; Szasz, 1984). In relation to coaching it is claimed that the expertise of a coach is related to the process rather than to the content of their work, and so is not as great as that of, say, a doctor or a teacher. The coach's expertise implies knowledge and skills that facilitate the coachee's learning. However, being an 'expert' of the process could still give the coach an opportunity to overstretch the coachee, to illustrate their intellectual power unnecessarily and to lead them in a direction that they have not chosen.

Coaches may also feel more powerful when they act as representatives of an organisation. This may lead them to associate themselves with the 'needs' of the organisation to such a degree that, for example, they put inappropriate pressure on their coachee to change, and in particular ways. The consequences of this action may enhance the reputation of the coach with their employer, but may have a negative impact on their relationship with their coachee and their long-term developmental process.

Among the psychological factors that may contribute to the coach's temptation to dominate are various personality traits, for example, Machiavellianism (Christie and Geis, 1970), dogmatism and locus of control (Lee-Chai *et al.*, 2001). There are also several power-related measures such as the Social Dominance Orientation scale (Pratto *et al.*, 1994) and the Misuse of Power scale (Lee-Chai *et al.*, 2001) that have been shown to be useful in research on power differentials. While acknowledging their value for such purposes, the emphasis of this chapter is on personal responsibility and the capacity to determine one's own behaviour.

If the coach takes seriously the issue of power as described here they will appreciate the need to examine their values and personal philosophy. This would include their very choice of coaching philosophy, for each philosophy (psychodynamic, cognitive-behavioural, person-centred, Gestalt, etc.) contains assumptions about power. And even if they are satisfied that their values and intentions are positive, they may yet wish to concede (with Freud, 1933; McClelland, 1987; Fitzgerald, 1993; Wilson and Brekke, 1994) that, on occasions, they may be unaware of their true motivations or even be subject to self-deception.

A particularly challenging account of human nature in relationship to power is found in the writings of Krishnamurti (1991, 1996). He invites us to look at our deepest psychological nature that is rarely free from social conditioning, typically glorifying success, power and competition. 'Power is another form of corruption – political power, religious power, power in the business world, power in the exercise of a certain talent that one has. . . . The energy, which is so necessary to bring about a transformation in the content of consciousness, is dissipated in all these ways' (Krishnamurti, 1996: 272). He leaves no doubt as to his attitude regarding the nature of power as explored in this chapter. 'Power in the sense of ascendancy, dominance, forceful influence over another, is evil at all times; there is no "good" power' (Krishnamurti, 1991: 182). This way of understanding power invites coaches to take an honest look at what is truly motivating them and how it may stand in the way of their best service to their coachees.

Contextual issues, including the power of the coachee

The coach clearly does not work in a vacuum with their coachee, but in a context that may include the organisation that buys their services, their representing company and their professional association. The question arises as to whether these relationships ever amount to impositions of will on the coach. Are *they* ever the victim of the power of others? In this section we sketch out some of the issues and the means by which this power may be exerted.

The coachee themselves may exert power over the coach in ways that vary in terms of consciousness and intent. At one extreme they may intimidate, mock or otherwise demean the coach, or, more covertly, may undermine their credibility by reporting unfavourably on their work, gossiping about them, wrongly attributing 'failure' to them or failing to attribute 'success' to them. Or they may simply underplay all positive aspects and focus only on minor difficulties (Clarkson, 2000). Furthermore, in the work itself, they may thwart the best endeavours of the coach; they may pace the process to their advantage, they may play on the perceived vulnerabilities of the coach, they may lead them into territory that is not of their choosing and resist attempts to move in the direction that is. At the end of the day they have considerable free will to go or not to go where they will and, if the coach is reluctant to follow, there is little he or she can do, ultimately, except follow or leave.

As mentioned earlier, there is a yet more subtle form of coachee power drawn paradoxically from the very value the coach may place on their work. To the extent, for example, that the coach values their reputation, the models and techniques they are working to, particular outcomes, etc., they become vulnerable to anyone who is in a position to deny them the outcomes they desire. In this case it is the coachee who may hold this power. The coach needs to keep a clear head not to become enthralled in an over-commitment to ends or means, but to remain open to the possibility of their non-fulfilment.

Another principal aspect of the context is the organisation for which the coach may be working. It is in a strong position to determine various aspects of the coaching practice, for example:

- The act of employment itself, with its control of access to the means of making and sustaining a livelihood, gives the employing agent considerable power over those seeking such a livelihood from them (Jackson and Carter, 2007).
- The organisation may instigate a coaching or mentoring programme that is closely wedded to the principal goals of the organisation, with specifically designed tasks itemised for attention and the deliberate exclusion of others (Klasen and Clutterbuck, 2002).
- The organisation may instigate a reporting framework to monitor activity and progress within the coaching encounter.
- The organisation is likely to allocate the space, time and facilities for the activity, with implications for the effectiveness of the work as well as the standing in which it is held.
- The organisation has the power to frame the activity in terms of staff expectations, which may affect the nature and potential of the work – anything from being a high-profile addition to a programme of personal development to a standard concession in a dismissal process.
- The organisation may regard the work as an adjunct to organisational change itself – an activity providing valuable feedback and focus for new ideas, or it may be treated as a discreet activity with no expectation of further effect.
- The organisation has access to the law and professional bodies of the coach whereby it may ensure that agreements are adhered to and deviations sanctioned.

- There may be a reporting mechanism back to the coaching organisation from which the coach came, with implications for their future employment.

There is also a more covert form of power that may be found in the language and logic with which organisational theory is constructed and in which coaches may find themselves enthralled, consciously or unconsciously. Morgan (2006: 4), for example, writes that 'all theories of organisations and management are based on implicit images or metaphors that lead us to see, understand, and manage (them) in distinctive yet partial ways'. He and other writers offer us metaphors for 'understanding' organisations – for example, as 'instruments of domination'. This may give rise to the idea that we have been beguiled by unchallenged concepts of 'rationality', which should be studied in the context of those who have a vested interest in their definition (Davies, 2005; Jackson and Carter, 2007). They also suggest, however, that times are changing and that the definitions themselves are now up for discussion, or should be. It is therefore expedient for coaches to be aware of whose definitions of 'reason', 'purpose' and 'value' they and their coachees are working to, and the mechanisms by which they have been brought about. As Hawkins and Smith (2006: 6) suggest, coaches need to be wary that their work does not 'become a tool that can be used to coerce individuals and groups to someone else's will, a will that they have no real chance of resisting, because it is dressed up in the clothes of "performance, efficiency and benefit to the organisation", or more directly impacts on whether they stay in their job'.

Standing this argument on its head for a moment, there is another notion here worthy of comment. Coaches may have a view of organisations that even leads them to avoid working in them because, for example, they feel they compromise the scope of their work beyond tolerable limits. How we view organisations will, in part, determine how we experience them. If for too long we have failed to see them as 'instruments of domination', we may yet want to avoid seeing them as only, or indeed principally, this. Morgan (2006) suggests other metaphors that may add yet more perspectives to our sight (for example, 'machines', 'organisms', 'brains' and 'psychic prisons'). It serves coaches well to keep their minds open to new ways of thinking – and ultimately to an awareness of the partiality of all thought. It would be ironic indeed if the most lasting thraldom they succumbed to was that of their own thinking.

Dealing with power in the immediacy of the coaching interaction

It is clear from the above that the consequences of power as domination are difficult to overestimate, both in terms of the broader view of the profession and in terms of the 'here and now' of the coaching interaction. In the case of the latter, we believe that it is awareness and consent that make the crucial difference between 'forceful influence' and 'imposition of will'. Some of the possible interplays are illustrated in Figure 8.1.

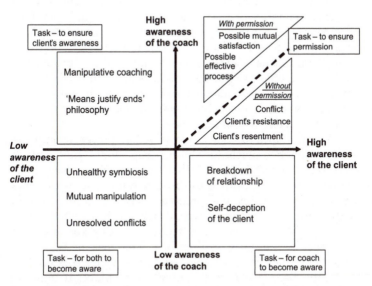

Figure 8.1 **Consent and awareness of power in the coaching relationship**

In the first quadrant the coach is aware of their imposition of will on the coachee but the coachee is not. Such a case might arise, for example, if the coach values outcome more highly than means. When the coach becomes aware of such a situation they have the option of drawing the coachee's attention to it and of involving them in the decision about the best way forward. Furthermore, it is expedient that they do this as soon as possible for, if Torbert's observation is correct, the value of any change thus evoked is likely to be highly questionable. 'Traditional forms of power, such as force, diplomacy, expertise or positional authority . . . may generate immediate acquiescence, conformity, dependence, or resistance. But . . . no matter in what combination, they will not generate transformation' (Torbert, 2004: 8).

When both the client and the coachee become aware of the possible use of power by the coach, the critical issue becomes a question of consent – whether explicit permission by the coachee is given (Quadrant 2). The coachee may give this permission willingly or they may do so under pressure of the need to change or in the belief that coaching has to have an element of challenge according to the principle of 'no pain – no gain'. They may even *ask* the coach to be tough with them. In this case the process may lead to mutual satisfaction and effective outcomes. It is important to notice, however, that this scenario implies that both the coachee and the coach are able to reconsider this arrangement at any point in the coaching engagement.

Another difficult scenario is when power is imposed on the coachee without their permission (Quadrant 2). Potential consequences of this are coachee resentment, overt or covert resistance to the coaching process or sometimes actual conflict. If expressed, these reactions could be healthy for the coachee's overall development. However, in some cases the coachee may 'resolve' this by keeping back the truth or actually telling lies. The loss of trust and rapport may be irrecoverable. And even when this conflict *is* openly discussed and 'learning' takes place, it may not justify the energy invested in getting that far. The way out for the coach is to check with their coachee if they ever sense they may be imposing their will on them and to adjust their behaviour as necessary.

The most problematic scenarios, however, are those in which the coach is unaware of their dominating behaviour (Quadrants 3 and 4). If the coachee also lacks awareness of this fact, it may not be discovered for some time, creating an unhealthy symbiosis or any one of many power games. In cases where the coachee becomes aware of such situations, they will probably choose to terminate the coaching relationship unless they have a good reason 'to play the game' on their own terms. It goes without saying that a coach would seek to avoid this situation.

The situations described in Figure 8.1 suggest that the awareness of the coach of exerting power on the coachee is a key factor that is likely to change the dynamics of the relationship. If the coach sees power in the terms described here and wishes to avoid its temptation, we believe that they need to be aware of its possibility moment by moment. They will then have the opportunity to stop or at least to raise the awareness of the coachee to the situation. The next step could be to seek the coachee's informed consent if there is any doubt as to its appropriateness. In the light of this debate, the first case that we started our chapter with is illustrative of power as imposition. The second case draws our attention to the crucial areas of awareness and consent, which require careful and open discussion. Where 'forceful influence' merges into 'imposition' may be analytically impossible to define, but when the consequences of getting it wrong can so impair the relationship on which hangs the value of the encounter, it is vital that the coach is as open and informed as possible.

Recommendations

We believe that the issue of power as domination has to be attended to by those who are responsible for coaching relationships and their long-term outcomes, i.e. by individual coaches, coaching companies, training providers and, in the most difficult legal and ethical cases, professional bodies.

There are two key dimensions to this issue – first, how to

identify and deal with any personal inclinations that one may find within oneself and, second, how to contend with the issue when met with in others. Here is a list of some ideas that have occurred to us in writing this chapter.

The three ancient 'golden rules' can hardly be bettered:

- Know thyself.
- Above all do no harm.
- Do nothing to anyone that you would not wish done to you.

More specifically we might add the following:

- *Keeping a distinct language for the analysis of power.* To examine this issue it is important to retain a distinct vocabulary, which avoids confusion with other uses of the same term.
- *Examining your personal philosophy in relation to power.* This implies having a clear understanding of how issues of power fit into your personal philosophy of life and work – how, for example, your very choice of theoretical tradition, models and techniques may have been influenced by your attitude to this phenomenon.
- *Developing self-knowledge.* This implies taking an honest look at yourself and how your attitude to power may have affected, and may still affect, your personal and professional relationships.
- *Developing self-awareness in the process of coaching.* It is important in understanding your own inclination to exercise power to monitor it moment by moment in the coaching encounter. For example, how do you normally introduce an activity that you want the coachee to take part in? Are you always transparent about the purpose of the activity? Do you give them enough information and time to make their choice to participate or not? How flexible or insistent are you on a particular interpretation of the outcomes of the activity? Even the common request to 'be reflective' may be an imposition unless the coachee truly understands and agrees to it.
- *Developing the capacity to stand firm when confronted with the real or imagined power of others.* This is always likely to involve a degree of courage, but courage often comes

with understanding. If we understand the potential for and nature of the phenomenon in ourselves, we may be less daunted when we meet it in others. This should mean that we are better placed to maintain the 'centeredness' (Hawkins and Smith, 2006: 246) we require to attend to the needs of our coachee.

- *Transparency with coachees.* If the coach feels that they are about to cross the line from influence to imposition (or indeed that the coachee is imposing their will on them), it is important that they discuss it with the coachee. As stated elsewhere, this may become a valuable learning experience for either or both parties, but most crucially, it safeguards the integrity of the process. Both the coachee and the coach have rights and responsibilities in this matter and it is vital that any hint of infringement is carefully discussed. If the coachee agrees to be 'pushed' it is even more important that the terms of the 'pushing' are understood, monitored and reviewed.
- *Sharing the concerns.* The subject of power is pervasive and elusive. If the coach finds that the issues in this chapter resonate with them, they would benefit from exploring them further with colleagues and supervisors.

We hope that the issues discussed in this chapter will help the coach to stay alert to the dangers of power in the coaching relationship. If Hobbes is right that the desire for power 'ceaseth only in death', we can at least seek to temper its prevalence in the meantime.

Reflective questions

- The point at which influence becomes an issue of power is difficult to determine. How might you reflect on this distinction in your own professional and private behaviour?
- Reflecting on your professional and private life, identify an occasion when someone or an organisation imposed their will on you. How did you feel and how did you react? What was the outcome?
- What steps can you take to minimise your own potential to exert power over others?

References

Bargh, J. and Alvarez, J. (2001) The road to hell: good intentions in the face of nonconscious tendencies to misuse power. In A. Lee-Chai and J. Baugh (eds) *The Use and Abuse of Power: Multiple Perspectives on the Causes of Corruption* (pp. 41–56). Hove: Psychology Press.

Christie, R. and Geis, F. (1970) *Studies in Machiavellianism*. New York: Academic Press.

Clarkson, P. (2000) *The Therapeutic Relationship*. London: Whurr Publishers.

Davies, B. (2005) The (im)possibility of intellectual work in neoliberal regimes. *Discourse: Studies in the Cultural Politics of Education*, 26: 1–14.

Fitzgerald, L. (1993) Sexual harassment: violence against women in the workplace. *American Psychologist*, 48: 1070–1076.

Freud, S. (1933) *New Introductory Lectures on Psychoanalysis* (Trans. W.J.H. Sprott). New York: Norton.

Fromm, E. (1960) *The Fear of Freedom*. London: Routledge.

Greene, R. (2006) *The 48 Laws of Power*. London: Profile Books.

Griffin, J. and Tyrrell, I. (2003) *Human Givens*. Chalvington: HG Publishing.

Gyllensten, K. and Palmer, S. (2007) The coaching relationship: an interpretative phenomenological analysis. *International Coaching Psychology Review*, 2: 168–177.

Hawkins, P. and Smith, N. (eds) (2006) *Coaching, Mentoring and Organizational Consultancy*. Maidenhead: Open University Press.

Hobbes, T. (1651) *Leviathan*. London: Clarendon Press.

Illich, I. (1971) *Disabling Professions*. London: Calder Publications.

Jackson, N. and Carter, P. (2007) *Rethinking Organisational Behaviour*. London: Prentice Hall.

Kilburg, R. (2004) Trudging toward Dodoville: conceptual approaches and case studies in executive coaching. *Consulting Psychology Journal: Practice and Research*, 56: 203–213.

Kipnis, D. (1984) Technology, power, and control. In S.B. Bacharach and E. Lawler (eds) *Sociology of Organizations*. Greenwich, ST: JAI Press.

Kipnis, D. (2001) Using power: Newton's Second Law. In A. Lee-Chai and J. Baugh (eds) *The Use and Abuse of Power: Multiple Perspectives on the Causes of Corruption* (pp. 3–18). Hove: Psychology Press.

Klasen, N. and Clutterbuck, D. (2002) *Implementing Mentoring Schemes*. London: Elsevier.

Krishnamurti, J. (1991) *Commentaries on Living, Third Series*. London: Victor Gollancz.

Krishnamurti, J. (1996) *Total Freedom: The Essential Krishnamurti*. New York: Harper Collins.

Lee-Chai, A., Shen, S. and Chartrand, T. (2001) From Moses to Marcos: individual differences in the use and abuse of power. In A. Lee-Chai and J. Baugh (eds) *The Use and Abuse of Power: Multiple Perspectives on the Causes of Corruption* (pp. 57–74). Hove: Psychology Press.

Lukes, S. (ed.) (1987) *Power*. Oxford: Basil Blackwell.

McClelland, D. (1987) *Human Motivation*. New York: Cambridge University Press.

Manathunga, C. (2007) Supervision as mentoring: the role of power and boundary crossing. *Studies in Continuing Education*, 29: 207–221.

Masson, J.M. (1989) *Against Psychotherapy*. London: Collins.

Milne, A.A. (2004) *When We Were Very Young*. London: Egmont.

Mitchell, T., Laarson, J. and Green, D. (1977) Leader behaviour, situational moderators, and group performance. *Organisational Behaviour and Human Performance*, 18: 254–268.

Morgan, G. (2006) *Images of Organisations*. London: Sage Publications.

O'Broin, A. and Palmer, S. (2007) Reappraising the coach–client relationship: the unassuming change agent in coaching. In S. Palmer and A. Whybrow (eds) *Handbook of Coaching Psychology: A Guide for Practitioners*. London: Routledge.

Pratto, F., Sidanious, J., Stallworth, I. and Malle, B. (1994) Social orientation: a personality variable predicting social and political attitudes. *Journal of Personality and Social Psychology*, 67: 741–763.

Ragins, B.R. (1997) Diversified mentoring relationships in organisations: a power perspective. *Academy of Management Review*, 22: 482–521.

Sampson, R.V. (1965) *Equality and Power*. London: Heinemann.

Sampson, R.V. (1985) *Society without the State*. London: Peace Pledge Union.

Schmidt, I. (1997) A motivational approach to the prediction of mentoring relationship satisfaction and future intention to mentor. Unpublished doctoral dissertation, University of Pittsburgh.

Spinelli, E. (1994) *Demystifying Therapy*. Ross-on-Wye: PCCS Books.

Szasz, T. (1984) *Myth of Mental Illness: Foundations of a Theory of Personal Contact*. London: Harper Colophon Books.

Torbert, W. (2004) *Action Inquiry: The Secret of Timely and Transforming Leadership*. San Francisco, CA: Berret-Koehler Publishers.

Wampold, B. (2001) *The Great Psychotherapy Debate: Models,*

Methods, and Findings. Mahwah, NJ: Lawrence Erlbaum Associates.

Wilson, T. and Brekke, N. (1994) Mental contamination and mental correction: unwanted influences on judgment and evaluations. *Psychological Bulletin*, 116: 117–142.

Zeig, J. (1980) *A Teaching Seminar with Milton H. Erickson.* New York: Brunner/Mazel.

Zimbardo, P.G. (1970) The human choice: individuation, reason and order versus de-individuation, impulse and chaos. In W.J. Arnold and D. Levine (eds) *Nebraska Symposium on Motivation* (pp. 237–307). Lincoln, NE: University of Nebraska Press.

Recommended books

Clarkson, P. (2000) *The Therapeutic Relationship.* London: Whurr Publishers.

Sampson, R.V. (1965) *Equality and Power.* London: Heinemann.

9

Last things first: ending well in the coaching relationship

Elaine Cox

Introduction

Two of the main reasons why coaches desire a good ending to their work are to provide customer satisfaction and gain repeat business. Marketing research has shown that endings occur when customers 'dissociate themselves from the object of their dissatisfaction' (Hirschman, 1970: 29) resulting in a switching of brand, reduction in consumption or the refusal to buy. To coaches, as professionals offering a service, a happy ending to the relationship is therefore paramount in order to satisfy and retain clients. Hodgetts (2002: 217), taking an organisational perspective, proposes that 'well-managed endings are just as essential to coaching success as clearly defined and explicit beginnings are'. If an ending is poorly managed, he argues, this can perpetuate an organisation's dependency on the coach. Hodgetts goes on to refer to the 'never-ending coaching engagement', suggesting that, like some therapy, coaching has the potential to go on indefinitely, and although there is probably learning to be had through continuation, in the organisational contract coaching is invariably tied to clear business strategies and objectives and usually ends once these objectives have been met. Thus, the ending is of significant practical importance not only to coachees wanting to achieve their aim, but also to the coach and the client organisation.

By understanding more about the nature of endings and the stages and factors involved in the process it is easier to anticipate potential issues and plan for a good ending. The purpose of this chapter, therefore, is to explore how a beneficial ending to the coaching alliance can be achieved. There are four sections. The first section compares the expectations of relationship endings in psychotherapy and counselling with those of coaching, and draws some lessons from the time-limited work of brief therapy. The second section introduces relationship stage models that have been developed in other spheres, beginning with Kram's mentoring phases model and then discussing a five-stage business-to-business relationship model (Tahtinen and Halinen, 2002), which also has implications for understanding and managing endings in coaching. This section also introduces the idea of predisposing and precipitating factors that impact on coaching at different stages. The third section provides case studies of three relationship endings in order to illustrate the importance of planned endings. In the final section the significance of the contracting process is discussed, from the importance of the initial stages through to review, in setting the parameters for the ending of the coaching.

Expectations of relationship endings in coaching and therapy

Much of the writing on endings in helping relationships is found in the areas of psychotherapy and counselling. In this section it is argued that coaching differs from therapy and counselling in three significant ways and that these impact on the way in which endings are construed. The first difference is in the level of interpretation by the coach.

Level of interpretation involved in the helping process

Ferraro (1995: 63) has suggested that the final phase in the psychoanalytic relationship is 'the most important interpretative act of the entire analysis'.

In therapy, as in psychoanalysis, the therapist holds a model of what the ending will look like, depending on the theoretical tradition in which he or she has been trained. For example, a gestalt trained therapist may be looking for increased awareness, less unfinished business, increased confidence, curiosity and a desire to experiment. These all show the therapist that the client has worked with their inner self to a degree acceptable to the therapist. Thus, there is an element of power vested in the therapist, provided by the theoretical model with which he/she is working. By contrast, coaching does not use specific theoretical frameworks to guide the work: coaches do not have a theoretical model that will lead them to be, as Murdin (2000: 3) says, 'waiting for specific indicators of readiness to end': the non-interpretive approach of coaching implies that the coach would follow the coachee's agenda right up to and including the decision to end the coaching. Coaches do not approach their work in an interpretive or analytic way; they eschew analysis and remain non-judgemental throughout.

It is useful for the coach to be aware of the danger that can occur when the professional does use a theoretical model that has inherent expectations of what constitutes progress towards an ending. In such cases he or she may construe a different view of the ending from that of the client. For example, as Murdin (2000: 5) points out, therapists can sometimes interpret a more complex patient story than is actually the case, basing their assumptions on the psychological theories with which they are familiar. In coaching, then, there should be a reduced danger of this: the coach takes what the coachee says at face value, using a non-judgemental (i.e. non-theoretical, non-analytic) approach. Belief by the coach that the coachee knows best facilitates the negotiation of an ending that can enable coachees to feel more powerful about influencing both the general event of ending in their lives and the specific ending in this coaching relationship. Giving the power to the coachee to end the relationship could be seen as one of the responsibilities of the coach.

Depth and exploitation of relationship

It is well documented that one of the key factors in achieving psychological change is the deliberate and active use of the in-depth relationship between therapist and patient (Frankel,

2007). In fact, Rogers (1961) described the therapeutic relationship itself as a growth experience. So the relationship is the therapy.

In the therapy and counselling literature, then, there is an emphasis on the relationship forged between helper and patient and the consequent feelings of loss that can result. The depth and quality of the relationship between therapist and client is seen as vitally important and the depth of that association has a significant impact on the ending of the relationship. Nevis (1996: 111), for example, points out that termination of the relationship is unusually important in the latter stages of therapy because it is the ending of a significant relationship and so the ending is 'the loss of a friend'. Murdin too mentions the 'hidden anxieties about loss' (2000: 37). Indeed, discussions of endings in the therapy and counselling literature all mention 'loss' as a significant factor. So, although therapy does not seek dependency, the fact that a close relationship is forged does lead to the potential for reliance on the therapist and therefore the potential to experience significant loss.

In coaching the relationship is important as well, but plays a different, less curative role: consequently it is often better to think of the coach/coachee relationship as a working alliance (Gavin, 2005). The goal of coaching is also different; it is not psychological change. Bachkirova (2007: 357) argues that the initial motivation for coaching is not the elimination of psychological problems or dysfunctions, but comes from the 'determination of the individual, supported or even stimulated by the organization, to improve performance'. Thus, the focus of coaching may be on change, but more often this is external change, which may result in some psychological change, but is not its main intention. The relationship, therefore, does not have the same function.

Time focus

The third way in which coaching differs from most therapy or counselling is in the way it is time-focused. In therapy and counselling, a time limit is generally not set, since the work will continue until the patient or client is 'better'. However, one form of therapy does make use of a shorter timeframe. Solution-focused brief therapy is an approach that has been found to be both rapid and effective. Drawing on a range of empirical research studies, the Brief Therapy Practice website (http://www.brief.org.uk) claims that Brief Therapy can bring about lasting change on average in less than five sessions and in up to 83 per cent of referrals. It can be brief because it is future-focused and works with the strengths of those who come by making the best use of their resources. It therefore brings about lasting change precisely because it aims from the outset to build solutions rather than solve problems.

Time limiting thus provides a form of impulsion for completion of the work and as Ledman (2004: 2) argues is one of the most potent tools available, since it provides the opportunity to work more 'consciously and constructively towards an ending from the very beginning'. The target date for ending may also be an impetus for a coachee to take more risks in experimenting with change. This emphasis on experimentation is captured in one of the key strategies in Brief Therapy – the Miracle Question (de Shazer, 1988): clients/coachees are asked to imagine that a miracle has occurred overnight and the problem that existed yesterday has gone away. They are asked to describe in detail what the day looks like now that the problem has ended and to focus on what the solution looks like, what specific behaviours indicate to them that the problem is solved. This enables the client to envisage the beginning of a new life without the problem and to focus on what life will be like after the work is completed.

Two End Plans

Significantly, Williams (1997: 339) argues in relation to psychotherapy that the ending is more than a final chapter and that the notion of ending operates as an influential organising principle from the start. She goes on to suggest that it has 'all the structuring and energising functions of an archetype in the human psyche', and explains how setting a time limit at the very start 'immediately and explicitly evokes the organising and energising force of the archetypal ending'. 'The ending always, but perhaps especially when it is invoked so deliberately as in time limited therapy, sets up an archetypal imperative – a rite of passage that propels the patient from an unconscious state into a conscious one' (1997: 340). For the coach, therefore, it is important to note the level of awareness that the invocation of ending invites for the coachee.

Williams (1997: 349) has identified a paradox for us in relation to the planning of endings. It could seem as if we can just 'sort out the aims, the criteria for concluding the work and we will know when and how to effect the ending'. However, it seems that the opposite is in fact true. The ending, when planned and regularly revisited, actually informs the criteria and process for the work and revises and updates the end. So the ending itself (or rather the explicit articulation and revision of it) becomes the means to the end.

The two 'End Plans' that might be played out in coaching are schematised in Figure 9.1. In this model the Means is the activity the coachee engages in with the intention of bringing about certain Ends[1] or goals. Ends have initially only an ideal existence, and the realised Ends, which are the actual outcomes of the adopted Means, may be quite different from the abstract Ends for which the Means were adopted at the outset.

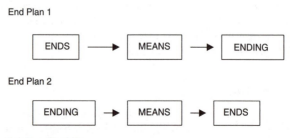

End Plan 1

ENDS ⟶ MEANS ⟶ ENDING

End Plan 2

ENDING ➡ MEANS ➡ ENDS

Figure 9.1 **Two End Plans**

---

[1] The Ends begin as very subjective ends: they reflect the desired changes in the objective world. Subsequently, they become realised Ends and are usually the unexpected results of the Means adopted.

In End Plan 1, the aims for the coaching are discussed and goals (Ends) set, but the actual Ending and what it might look like is not explored in any detail. It is assumed that this will happen after six/twelve sessions when the contract ends or goals have been met. This results in vagueness and uncertainty about the ending of the coaching, and could lead to a range of dilemmas (see Case Study 3 later in this chapter).

In End Plan 2, however, the Ending of the coaching is planned and the world after coaching is described and discussed in detail from the outset. This enables a meaningful discussion of how the Ends are to be achieved and an adequate conception of the Ending becomes a powerful Means in its own right. An example of End Plan 2 is played out in Case Study 2.

Relationship stage models

Endings of relationships have been recognised as part of a dynamic, constructive process that moves through a number of recognised stages that define the changes as the relationship matures. This section outlines a number of models that demonstrate the importance of the stages of relationships and highlight how attention to the development of the relationship through each of the phases can help prevent some of the issues involved in securing a successful ending.

Kram studied mentors in the workplace during the 1980s and her work identifies a number of phases of the mentor relationship. She describes the initiation phase as the period when the relationship begins and includes two possible ending phases: separation and redefinition (Kram, 1988: 49). Separation, Kram suggests, denotes a significant change in the structural factors and/or the emotional experience of the relationship (including disruption and loss). This change may involve the mentee achieving more autonomy or the mentor being less available to provide the mentoring function. It may also include practical or organisational impediments to continuation. The second of Kram's ending phases involves a redefinition of the relationship. This is particularly important in peer relationships where the mentor and mentee need to maintain an ongoing working relationship once the mentoring has ended.

Building on Kram's model, Megginson and Clutterbuck (1995: 4–5) listed the dynamic processes of the phases of the relationship. The particular dynamic of the 'moving on' or ending stage is captured in Table 9.1.

In the moving-on stage it is interesting to note that mentors need to deal with feelings of 'rupture and loss'. The mentoring relationships studied by Kram were typically two to five years in length and Kram suggests that termination was crucial to protégés' sense of independence. This suggests that the close relationship built between mentor and protégé over a long period can sometimes lead to dependency and needs careful management.

Clutterbuck and Megginson (2004) have also researched the endings of mentoring relationships and made the distinction between 'winding up' and 'winding down'; the former being a proactive approach and the latter being a gradual drifting apart. The findings of this study indicate that there are a number of factors to consider in regard to ending the relationship, including preparing the mentee for the ending, recognising the changes in the relationship, for example where energy or motivation appears to be changing, and reviewing the relationship regularly in order to provide a forum for discussion of a potential ending.

Table 9.1 The ending stage in the life-cycle of a mentoring relationship

Stage	Mentor and mentee tasks	Dynamics of the relationship	Skills required by the mentor
Moving on	• allow relationship to end or evolve • move to maintenance • review what can be taken and used in other contexts	• dealing with rupture and loss • major renegotiation and continuation • evaluation and generalisation	• address own and others' feelings of loss • develop next phase and/or orchestrate a good ending • think through and generalise learning • establish friendship

The majority of professional coaches work in some form of organisational setting and so an understanding of business-based models is also important. Tahtinen and Halinen (2002: 172) have divided the process of business relationships into seven stages: assessment, decision making, dyadic communication, network communication, disengagement, aftermath and restoring stages of a relationship. Each stage describes the decisions and actions that managers perform in it, but the number and order of the stages may vary from case to case.

Heffernan's (2004) business-to-business model is also interesting since it begins with a 'pre-relationship stage', which can identify predisposing factors. Heffernan (2004: 117) argues that the amount of learning that transpires at the Early Interactions phase is at its highest level of any stage of the relationship life-cycle and that lack of understanding at this phase can make the relationship fragile. At the Relationship growth stage there is a high level of engagement and interaction between parties, plus intensive mutual learning towards the specifics of the relationship. Learning achieved at this stage could reduce the uncertainty and distance between coach and coachee. The Partnership stage is the relationship at its most mature and partners have developed a high level of experience in dealing with each other. Finally, the Relationship end stage is 'how partners "uncouple" the relationship because the purpose of the relationship no longer exists'. Heffernan (2004: 17) also suggests that 'a relationship can be terminated at any stage of the relationship lifecycle; however, the relationship end stage comes about when the reason for the relationship is no longer current'. He goes on to describe how trust is the most critical aspect to develop at the initial stages and this has an impact on the potential of the relationship to develop through to a natural end stage where purposes have been met.

This section has outlined relationship stages in order to stress the changing process that informs the alliance between coach and coachee. It is also important to highlight that, as the models suggest, the ending of the relationship is prefigured in the early stages of the alliance.

Predisposing and precipitating factors

Heffernan's five-stage model, discussed above, begins by identifying factors that affect the alliance. Similarly, there are issues that may arise before and during coaching which cause or have an impact on the end of the relationship. It is useful, therefore, to think of these issues either as predisposing (inherent in the coach or coachee as individuals before the coaching begins) or as precipitating (arising during the coaching engagement from developments in the lives of the coachee or the coach, the relationship between them or indeed the client organisation). Some examples are given below.

Predisposing factors

- A coachee presents for coaching with issues that are evidently more suited to counselling or therapy. If coaching were to go ahead it would very likely be affected by the inappropriateness of the issue and result in premature ending.
- The coach feels anxiety about the ending, believing that the coachee may not 'manage'. It has become obvious to the coach that the coachee is not going to be ready to end at the end date. Although it seems that this may be a precipitating factor, in fact the coach's anxiety may be as a result of inexperience, holding firm to inappropriate theories, or the coach may have ongoing issues that need to be worked through. There may also be an element of perfectionism on the part of the coach in wanting to get it 'right' for the coachee. These are issues to be discussed in supervision.
- Inexperienced coaches may encounter problems in dealing with resistance and this could provoke them to make a premature ending. They may feel they are not getting anywhere and consider referral, believing the coachee to have a therapeutic need.

Precipitating factors

- Coachees often encounter practical difficulties, such as new time commitments, job challenges, changes in child-care arrangements etc. The difficulties may be real but can also indicate something difficult in the coaching relationship itself. The coach will need to listen for underlying feelings that may be indirectly expressed; is this a strategy for opting out of the coaching alliance or is there something important that is not being expressed, but needs to be addressed in coaching? A review meeting is vital for addressing these issues.

- Precipitating factors need not always be related to external changes; sometimes precipitating factors can uncover predispositional factors that need psychological work to achieve change. In this case the coach is advised to refer the client for therapy or counselling. For example, the coachee (or the coach) may have become dependent on the relationship and fears loss. Consequently, there is an avoidance of the ending. In this case, it may be necessary to refer the client, but coaches should also think about responses to endings in their own lives and discuss this in supervision. Coaches sometimes have unfinished psychological issues of their own, which may impinge on their ability to end the relationship. They may, for example, have a real need to be validated as successful in terms of 'full-term' coaching assignments.
- Rarely, events may occur during the coaching that cause concern from an ethical point of view. Such concerns would need addressing in a review meeting and a solution or ending sought. It is also important for the coach to uphold ethical standards. For example, maintaining a failing relationship is possible where the coach has a lucrative contract with the client organisation and where a premature or unsatisfactory ending is seen as failure and may result in termination of the contract. So the coach has a financial agenda that is in conflict with the client's wellbeing. Regular supervisor support would seem vital here in order to raise coach awareness.
- Organisational change may occur during the coaching that makes it impractical or impossible to continue the coaching. If an organisation is involved with the coaching contract then a three-way review will be necessary.

Case studies

The following real case studies illustrate three different types of endings and highlight a number of the issues discussed so far.

Case Study 1 – Sylvio

This case is an example of a close, informal mentoring-type relationship that had an unsatisfactory and seemingly premature ending. There is evidence of dependency and the expectation on my part that this was an enduring friendship.

Sylvio and I had a relationship that developed through an initial 'pen-friend' exchange. We wrote regular, long letters where we discussed issues in our lives and each of us would offer our own experiences, suggestions for reading and ask questions aimed at guiding or informing the other in the resolution of dilemmas and concerns. As well as corresponding regularly, we also had several telephone conversations and two or three face-to-face meetings. Both of us had some major personal and work-related issues to confront and there were uncomfortable, life-changing decisions that we each needed to make. The correspondence was useful in provoking thinking in all of these areas. However, no ending to the relationship was ever discussed, and although we did review and discuss the relationship itself fairly often, no End Plan was ever made.

Consequently, when the ending with Sylvio came and was very sudden and totally unplanned, it was, for me, highly unsatisfactory. He wrote a comparatively short letter to say that he would no longer be writing and that I was not to contact him. The suddenness and lack of preparation left me with acute feelings of loss and afterwards I could only speculate about the reasons for the ending. Such speculations are inevitable when there is lack of clarity and certainty and are not helpful.

This was not a professional relationship and so there was no inevitability about its ending at all. Had it been a coaching relationship it would have been set up differently and especially important would have been the initial assessment of the work needed to identify any predisposing factors. A review process would also have been key in order to ensure that referral could be effected if necessary. In addition, it would have been the coach's responsibility to ensure a positive ending experience and so avert harmful speculation and possibly break negative response patterns.

Case Study 2 – Graham

Case Study 2 is an example of a coaching alliance with a time set for ending at the outset. It is an example of End Plan 2 and shows that a planned ending informs the means of attainment and the ultimate realised end.

Graham came to me for coaching because he was one year away from retirement and wanted to prepare both mentally and physically for leaving work. The retirement date was the fixed ending for the coaching assignment and a detailed assessment was made, which showed a clear coaching need. Contracting included a specific picturing of how the ending would look and feel and what days would be like after the ending. We even envisaged the retirement party. Graham and I worked together throughout the year to examine what his contribution had been to his organisation and what might fill the gap after retirement. We looked at existential issues connected with withdrawal from the workplace as well as the financial and practical issues of retirement.

In this coaching alliance the ending date drove the coaching, providing both a timescale in which to operate and plan and also a focus for exploring beyond. The time constraint also gave Graham ownership of the process: even though there was a full year for the coaching work, his deadline was real and this impacted favourably on the clarity of the coaching work.

The following is an example of the kind of dialogue that took place and illustrates Graham's detailed descriptions of what life will be like after the coaching has ended. Graham wanted to be purposeful in his retirement, but not constrained by a routine. We were working to explore what purposeful meant for him.

COACH: So describe how you are beginning an ordinary
            day, a weekday, one month after you have left
            work. Give me as much detail as you can.

GRAHAM: Well, I get up, probably later than I do now
            and get dressed and I have a leisurely break-
            fast with time for some toast and two cups of
            coffee.

COACH: How are you feeling now – during breakfast?
            *[Notice that I am asking questions as though
            breakfast is happening now. This brings the
            End closer to our current conversation, which is
            the Means].*

GRAHAM: It feels decadent, but it's what I enjoy, so I don't
            feel guilty – not like if I was supposed to be at
            work and I was making myself late.

COACH: What are you doing after breakfast?

GRAHAM: I am walking to the shop to get a paper and
            then back in time to listen to the radio at 9 am.
            I'm also thinking it would be good to have a
            dog.

COACH: So it is still quite early. What are you listening
            to on the radio? Is it music?

GRAHAM: No, it's Radio 4. At 9 am each day they have
            very interesting programmes that I can't listen
            to when I'm at work.

COACH: How does listening to the programme make you
            feel? *[I ask about feelings to help Graham recog-
            nise the affective aspects of the choices that he
            makes during this day. This will confirm right-
            ness or otherwise.]*

GRAHAM: I feel great. I feel I am doing something I always
            wanted to do. It's a bit like the breakfast feel-
            ing. So it's decadent if that doesn't sound silly.
            I'm not sure if it will always feel like that – as it
            gets more familiar it may just feel normal.

COACH: How important is it to be 'decadent' and doing
            the things you always wanted to do?

GRAHAM: Very important because for years I've lived for
            my work and my life has felt as though it's been

on hold. Now I want to do some of the things
I've not been able to do.

COACH: You mentioned you are thinking it would be
            good to have a dog. How will that be good?

GRAHAM: It will put some routine in my day. Even though
            I said I don't want routine it is still good to
            have some responsibility. A dog will make me
            take more walks and it will be company. I have
            a big garden, and everything is in place.

COACH: Sounds like he has a good home. What sort of
            dog is he?

GRAHAM: I've always wanted a spaniel. Not too big, but
            not too small.

COACH: We've moved away from describing your day.
            Tell me what happens after the radio pro-
            gramme has ended. *[Here I've moved Graham
            away from the conversation about the dog,
            although I definitely pick up on it again later as
            it seems as if this will provide some purpose in
            his retirement. But we also need to explore the
            rest of the day in order to find out what else
            Graham feels that he wants.]*

This dialogue illustrates how talking about what life
will be like after coaching shifts the focus of the relationship
away from what to do in our here and now in order to achieve
perceived outcomes, to what it is actually like to live in the
new world. Real goals and objectives seem to 'fall out' of the
discussion naturally and in context, rather than having to be
thought up or contrived in response to my direct questioning.

Case Study 3 – William

The third case study is an example of a coaching alliance
where an ending was not explicitly planned. The GROW
model was used (Goals, Reality, Options, Will) (West and
Milan, 2001) to structure the coaching, but the alliance
culminated in a premature ending with feelings of dissatisfaction and uncertainty for both coach and coachee.

William came for coaching with a goal of wanting to be

successful in his career, so at assessment a coaching need was identified. More exploration revealed that a high salary characterised his idea of success. However, when we looked at the reality there was a mismatch between what he enjoyed doing in his work and the amount of money he knew he could realistically earn to support his family. This, together with certain other blocks that we gradually identified over the first three meetings, would all impinge on his earning capacity. Contracting had included planning a scheduled review to look at what had been achieved and to decide how many further sessions would be needed, but no specific date for ending the coaching was set and we did not explore in detail what a successful ending would look like or what life would look like afterwards.

At the fourth meeting we reviewed progress so far and it seemed evident that no tangible steps had been taken towards achievement of the goal, although some of the clarification had been useful. The review revealed that a number of precipitating factors in William's personal life meant that his goal of earning more money became more urgent. This imperative meant that there was little scope to experiment and little time to spend on the coaching. At the review there was no mention of the ending date, nor was there any discussion of what the ending would look like. We had only reviewed what had been achieved and the currency of the goal. It was at this point that the coaching finished prematurely.

This is an example of End Plan 1 in operation, and it is my belief that had a specific ending been designed then the Means to William's Ends (goals) would have become clearer. In addition, if we had explored a typical day after the end of the coaching, as illustrated in the dialogue with Graham, then useful insights into William's real goals would have been achieved.

Part of the remit of the coach working with GROW is to help the client create SMART goals (Specific, Measured, Achievable, Realist and Timed). In this scenario, William's goal was difficult to break down in this way, but it could be argued that the timed element in that model is the most important and if addressed sufficiently at the start of coaching, when goals are being discussed, it will help achieve the focus and imperative necessary.

In the three examples given above, there was no contract with a client organisation. However, it is important to highlight that if the coach fails to consider endings with all parties including the organisational client when appropriate, then the ending phase may be rushed or dismissed as not important, with disappointing consequences. It is, therefore, just as important to have a detailed discussion of the end with the client organisation as with the coachee.

The contracting process

Throughout this chapter the interrelating stages of the coaching alliance have been indicated. Figure 9.2 summarises the contracting *process*. From this figure, it can be noted

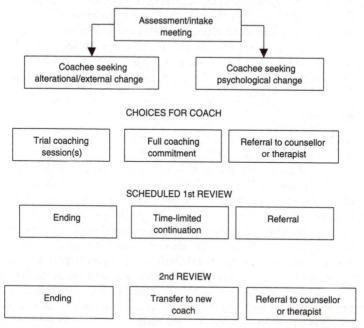

Figure 9.2 The contracting process

that the initial assessment and intake meeting is a vital foundation for the establishment of the coaching alliance, but the reviews that take place later are also important in reinforcing commitment and realigning the coaching work, and so they too become part of the contracting process. There are therefore three stages to the process: assessment/intake, review and ending.

Assessment/intake

Problems in ending the relationship may relate to the kind of problem that the coachee brings in the first place. So, careful assessment is important. The initial assessment ensures that the expectations of the coachee (and organisational client) can be met and any predisposing factors taken into account. If the potential coachee is seeking or needing psychological help, for example, or it is apparent that they want mentoring or advice and guidance, then referral can be made. Following assessment the coach then has the choice, either to contract with the coachee (and organisational client) in some way, or to refer to another professional. Thus, it can be seen that the ethical and professional stance of the coach is evident from the outset and is already impacting on the potential ending.

Review

Also inbuilt into the contracting process are review meetings. The review is vital because it means that there is a safeguard for an 'unproductive' relationship or one thwarted by precipitating factors, as discussed earlier. When a scheduled review is contracted it provides an 'escape lane' for both coach and coachee. After this point has been reached, further coaching needs can be negotiated and the ending re-envisaged. If there is no perceived benefit in extending, discussion focuses on what will be accomplished in the remaining time, or on planning for an imminent ending. An evaluation meeting with the coachee's organisation at around the same time might focus on alternative developmental opportunities for the coachee.

A coach should not assume that the coachee shares the

same feelings towards the ending. Their initial agreement and certainty about an end date may have changed over the period of the coaching. At the review stage the coach has the opportunity for a formal check of whether the coachee needs the same ending and the same timing and to re-describe and plan the ending. So a review meeting may also provide an opportunity to redirect or redeem the coaching alliance and negotiate a different contract. Sometimes it can lead to a decision to create a 'faded' ending where there is a gradual withdrawal of regular meetings.

Ending

It can be seen how it is better for the ending to be jointly conceived (or theorised) by the coachee and the coach at the start of the coaching assignment. In fact, just as the nature of the coaching itself is mutually defined at the assessment stage, so the 'specific indicators of readiness to end' can be pinpointed jointly before the coaching begins. It is thus argued here that the whole of the coaching encounter should be defined in the contracting space, including the ending. Ending is part of the contract and so it is vital to end well, ethically and on time.

In addition, the ending itself plays an important part in the work together and should be carefully planned so that it can consolidate what has been achieved and aid the generalisation of learning into new situations. Arguably, one of the goals of coaching is to encourage autonomy in the coachee plus the ability to self-coach. In fact, Ingram (2003: 531) suggests that 'recapitulation of the work in the final sessions can create a sense of narrative flow which permanently and consciously internalises the experience'. The role of the coach therefore is to ensure that the client has the opportunity to review the coaching experience and to develop an 'exit strategy'. Part of that strategy will be to build self-efficacy and to encourage self-sufficiency and self-coaching throughout, thus helping the coachee to recognise that they have the potential within them to succeed alone.

Nevertheless, however carefully the coach has contracted with the coachee and planned the ending, a less than successful ending can sometimes occur. There are three ways in which this can occur:

- Williams (1997: 345) has suggested that in therapy, the emotional pressure of the impending separation some-times acts as a 'catalyst to reactivate anxieties that have not been fully worked through'. When this happens at the end of an otherwise successful coaching engagement, and depending on the nature of the anxieties, this may be a case for referral to a therapist, counsellor or another coach.
- In a second example, the coach is an active participant in early termination because for some reason the coaching has become untenable and referral is desired. The sugges-tion should be made to the coachee with reasons why ending appears necessary. If the coachee agrees, there is discussion of the most appropriate way to conclude. If the coachee does not agree, then the very act of suggesting referral may prove to be an effective intervention.
- In the final example, it is the coachee who has decided that he or she no longer requires coaching. However, in this instance a formal ending is also important. A clear, well-planned ending provides closure for the coach and a positive model for the coachee. It helps to avoid the specu-lation and feelings encountered in Case Study 1.

Conclusion

Having contracted, planned for and reached the endings stage in the way described above, it is more likely that the coach/coachee will experience the kind of ending antici-pated. Nevertheless, it is useful to consider the process again briefly in relation to the feelings that may arise for coach and coachee at the end of the relationship. The degree of these feelings should not be as intense as in the ending of a close personal relationship, but nevertheless they are important to recognise and work through, preferably together. As dis-cussed earlier, if the ending is planned and celebrated as an integral part of the working alliance then feelings of loss will be minimal. If a review stage is programmed in to the process and the relationship has to be ended prematurely for some reason then there will be less anger or self-blame and less sadness and guilt. If unhelpful feelings are experienced then the coach should discuss these with a supervisor. It is also the responsibility of the coach to ensure that the coachee is not left with unexamined negative feelings at the end of the coaching, and so it is vital that the issues are talked through and some form of ongoing support arranged, through either the client organisation or referral to another coach or to a therapist or counsellor.

An ending marks a threshold that must be crossed and the possibility of a new beginning. Although completing the coaching process itself cannot usually be seen as a 'rite of passage' (except sometimes for the novice coach), often the achievement of the ends/goals for the coachee are of great importance to them. A rite of passage according to Williams (1997: 340–41) makes it evident that 'something of great significance has been taking place within the individual which has now come to fruition and must be celebrated [. . .] consolidating what has been achieved and indicating what yet lies ahead to be dared and mastered'. Coachees may achieve promotions or new employment offers as a result of the coaching, or they may realise change in their approach to self-management or their relationships. Any of these achievements may feel like a rite of passage and each will be worthy of celebration. In Graham's case, a plan for a successful retirement was the goal, but celebration was also part of the grand plan for the ending of our coaching relationship.

If the ending is not discussed, planned and celebrated and the relationship is left to fade or to end abruptly without closure, then the potential for marking achievement and fully integrating changes may be lost.

Reflective questions
- What evidence do we have that the limits or finitude of things is written into the archetypal blueprint of our lives?
- How can attention to the development of the coaching alliance through stages help build a good ending?
- What is the nature of the gap coaching leaves, if it does not involve loss?

References

Bachkirova, T. (2007) Role of coaching psychology in defining boundaries between counselling and coaching. In S. Palmer and A. Whybrow (eds) *Handbook of Coaching Psychology: A Guide for Practitioners*. London: Routledge.

Clutterbuck, D. and Megginson, D. (2004) All good things must come to an end: winding up and winding down a mentoring relationship. In D. Clutterbuck and G. Lane (eds) *The Situational Mentor: An International Review of Competences and Capabilities in Mentoring*. Aldershot: Gower.

de Shazer, S. (1988) *Clues: Investigating Solutions in Brief Therapy*. New York: Norton.

Feltham, C. (1997) *Time Limited Counselling*. London: Sage.

Ferraro, F. (1995) Trauma and termination. *International Journal of Psycho-Analysis*, 76: 51–65.

Frankel, S. (2007) *Making Psychotherapy Work*. Madison, CT: Psychosocial Press.

Gavin, J. (2005) *Lifestyle Fitness Coaching*. Leeds: Human Kinetics Europe Ltd.

Heffernan, T. (2004) Trust formation in cross-cultural business-to-business relationships. *Qualitative Market Research: An International Journal*, 7: 114–125.

Hirschman, A.O. (1970) *Exit, Voice, and Loyalty: Responses to Decline in Firms, Organizations and States*. Cambridge, MA: Harvard University Press.

Hodgetts, W. (2002) Using executive coaching in organisation. In C. Fitzgerald and J. Garvey Berger (eds) *Executive Coaching*. Mountain View, CA: Davies-Black Publishing.

Ingram, G. (2003) Ending and the nature of therapeutic time: examples from art, culture and brief therapy. *Psychodynamic Practice*, 9: 521–545.

Kram, K. (1988) *Mentoring at Work*. London: University Press of America.

Ledman, S. (2004) *Satisfactory Endings*. BACP Information Sheets: 10.

Megginson, D. and Clutterbuck, D. (1995) *Mentoring in Action*. London: Kogan Page.

Murdin, L. (2000) *How Much Is Enough?* London: Routledge.

Nevis, E. (1996) *Gestalt Therapy: Perspectives and Application*. London: Routledge.

Rogers, C. (1961) *On Becoming a Person: A Therapist's View of Psychotherapy*. London: Constable.

Tahtinen, J. and Halinen, A. (2002) Research on ending exchange relationships: a categorization, assessment and outlook. *Marketing Theory*, 2: 165–188.

West, L. and Milan, M. (eds) (2001) *The Reflecting Glass*. London: Palgrave.

Williams, S. (1997) Psychotherapeutic ends and endings. *British Journal of Psychotherapy*, 13: 337–350.

Recommended books

Feltham, C. (1997) *Time Limited Counselling*. London: Sage.

Murdin, L. (2000) *How Much Is Enough?* London: Routledge.

Walsh, J. and Meenaghan, T. (2007) *Endings in Clinical Practice*. Chicago, IL: Lyceum Books.

10

Coaching relationships and ethical practice

Ho Law

Introduction

For coaches, it is generally recognised that ethical practice is important to coaching relationships. However (and amazingly), there is a noticeable absence of the topic of ethics in conversation among coaches and coachees. The number of participants in coaching workshops at conferences is relatively small in comparison with the attendees at workshops on marketing and general coaching techniques, for example 'how to run your coaching business', 'inspirational leadership' or 'positive psychology'. It appears as if there is some degree of apathy about ethics in action, the assumption being that coaches should know best. Myths abound about coaching ethics. It is as if 'ethics is simply to do what's right'. The author is not suggesting that there is a lack of ethical practice in coaching, but argues a case that coaches may need more practical information about ethics in coaching. This chapter aims to fill the void of practical coaching ethics for coaches and stakeholders (customers, coachees or coaching buyers). It first defines what ethics are. It then argues how and why they matter in coaching and describes the ethical guidelines that are provided by various professional bodies. The chapter then goes on to describe the challenges in coaching relationships – problems/difficulties that can arise in the relationship between the coach, the coachee and their organisation. It also provides a case study to demonstrate a typical coaching dilemma and how it affects the coaching relationship. This is followed by a discussion on how to ensure an ethical approach in real-life practice in coaching such as using modern technology such as broadband, emails, web cameras. Finally a summary of key concepts is provided.

Definition of ethics

Many business leaders, coaches and managers believe that ethics simply involves 'learning what is right or wrong, and then doing the right thing' (McNamara, 2008). One would have thought that the definition of ethics would be quite clear and non-ambiguous. However, this is not so true. A quick search on the Internet on the definition of ethics provides a very diverse range of definitions ranging from a simple code of 'right' and 'wrong' to different religious views.

The term 'ethics' (or *ethik* in Middle English or *ethique* in Old French) has Indo-European roots. It originated from the Greek *ethikos* (ethical) as in ethos. The modern definitions of ethics include:

- 'The principles of right and wrong that are accepted by an individual or a social group' (*Wordnet*, 2008).
- 'The study of the general nature of morals and of the specific moral choices to be made by a person; *moral philosophy*' (*The Free Dictionary*, 2008).
- 'The rules or standards governing the conduct of a person or the members of a profession' (*The Free Dictionary*, 2008), such as medical ethics or in this context, coaching ethics.

The term is closely associated with 'ethical code, ethical motive, and moral philosophy', where the ethical code is 'a system of principles governing morality and acceptable conduct'; ethical motive the 'motivation based on ideas of right and wrong'; and moral philosophy 'the philosophical study of moral values and rules' (*Collins Essential Thesaurus*, 2006; *Wordnet*, 2008: http://wordnet.princeton.edu).

The term also implies that there is 'a code of behaviour', which is specific to a particular professional group, such as business or medical ethics. Thus, the key questions for coaches and coachees are:

- What are 'coaching ethics'?
- What are their implications to the coaching relationship in practice?

The concept of ethics is viewed by scholars as a major branch of philosophy. It is regarded as significantly broader than the common conception of analysing right and wrong. It encompasses not only 'the right conduct', but also 'the good life' – the life worth living or life that is simply not just satisfying. This concept is held by many philosophers to be more important than moral conduct (Singer, 1993). This view has important implications to coaching, especially life coaching.

This chapter focuses on the practical implication of ethics in coaching and the coaching relationship in particular by adopting Rowson's (2001) definition of ethical principle. Within the coaching context, ethical practices are defined as applying the *rules* that coaches are *committed* to because they see them as embodying their *values* and *justifying* their *moral judgements*. This definition can then be translated into 'a sequence of cognitive processes' (Law, 2006):

Morality $\Rightarrow$ professional judgement $\Rightarrow$ rationale $\Rightarrow$ values $\Rightarrow$ commitment $\Rightarrow$ rules

In practice, doing 'the right thing' according to the above process is not always as straightforward. We shall explore further in the following sections how the above process may influence the coaching relationship.

Ethical guidelines from various professional bodies

Ethics in the professional bodies are usually managed through the use of codes of ethics and standards of practices. Ethical guidelines are included in many professional bodies as a form of self-regulation, where their members are expected to commit to ethical standards and codes of practice. The professional coaching bodies include:

- The Association for Coaching (AC)
- The Association for Professional Executive Coaching and Supervision (APECS)

- The British Psychological Society and its section Special Group in Coaching Psychology (BPS, SGCP)
- The European Mentoring and Coaching Council (EMCC)
- The International Coach Federation (ICF)
- The Society for Coaching Psychology (SCP)

In general, the coaching professional body provides members with the code of ethics and practice. Most of the above bodies expect their members to recognise both personal and professional limitations in their practice with reference to the number of requirements as a code of practice. The EMCC categorises its Ethical Code into the following aspects:

- competence
- context
- boundary management
- integrity
- professionalism.

The BPS *Code of Ethics and Conduct* provides general guiding principles for psychologists. These are based on the following four principles of ethics:

- respect
- competence
- responsibility
- integrity.

The code further expands each principle with a 'Statement of Values'. This reflects the deeper cognitive aspects of understanding the value of ethics in terms of individual 'beliefs'. According to our rule of engagement described in the definition section ('a sequence of cognitive processes'; Law, 2006), this has an important implication for decision making. Each ethical principle is further explained in terms of a set of standards.

Although the BPS *Code of Ethics and Conduct* has provided the four overarching ethical principles that set explicit standards and implicitly inform behaviours, it does not include a detailed code of practice. This may be due to the diverse applications of psychology. Offering explicit advice for every possible interaction would be impossible. For example, the practices of clinical psychologists are very different from coaching psychologists. There are also a large number of psychologists working in academia whose primary engagement is conducting research. Thus, many coaching psychologists in private practice would find the *Good Practice Guidelines for the Conduct of Psychological Research within the NHS* as irrelevant. On the other hand, the *Guidelines for Professional Practice in Counselling Psychology* may be a useful guide for coaching psychologists. It describes the practitioner's responsibilities at three levels:

1 to self and to clients;
2 to self and to colleagues;
3 to self and to society.

For psychologists practising coaching, they have to draw together diverse sets of guidelines, filter out the relevant materials, and translate them into their own context – this is quite a daunting task!

In practice, it may be more appropriate to link the code of practice to ethics in terms of the coaching values and principles. From this viewpoint, the code can be categorised into six ethical principles, which the author has called the 6 R's of ethical principles (which have been adopted as the *Code of Ethics and Practice* for the Society for Coaching Psychology):

• rights
• respect
• recognition
• relationship
• representation
• responsibility.

The six ethical principles are interrelated, especially the principles of rights and respect, which are so interwoven in practice that they can be combined into a single principle. The code of practice under the above headings can be summarised as follows:

Rights and respect – respect the rights of the coachee as a human being

- Coaching contract – provide the client with an explicit contract at the outset of a coaching programme (e.g. AC, SCP).
- Confidentiality – maintain confidentiality of the coachee and/or client (e.g. BPS, EMCC, SCP).
- Respect the client's right (e.g. AC, APECS, EMCC, BPS, SCP).
- Informed consent – obtain informed consent for using the information about the coachee for various purposes (e.g. BPS, SCP).
- Diversity – be sensitive to the coachee's individual and cultural difference such as age, gender, disability, race, religion/belief, sexual orientation, etc. (e.g. AC, APECS, BPS, SCP).
- Openness – be open to respond to the client's requests for information (e.g. AC, EMCC, APECS).

Recognition – recognise the standards and limits of one's own competence

- Professional competency – practice within the boundaries of competence (e.g. BPS, EMCC, ICF, SCP).

Relationship – establish a good relationship and trust with the coachee/client

- Dual/multiple relationships – clarify multiple roles and resolve conflicts (e.g. AC, APECS, EMCC, ICF, SCP).

Representation – represent oneself and the profession accurately and honestly

- Represent oneself and the profession appropriately – act in a manner that does not bring the profession of coaching into disrepute (e.g. AC, BPS, EMCC, ICF, SCP).

Responsibility – take professional responsibility for oneself and one's coachees/clients, the stakeholders and the society

- Responsibility to the coachee – encourage the coachee to take responsibility for their own learning (e.g. SCP).
- Responsibility to oneself – apply and evaluate coaching outcomes; keep appropriate records of coaching practice; maintain continuous professional development and supervision; have professional indemnity insurance (e.g. AC, APECS, EMCC, BPS, SCP).

Note that the ICF summarises the code of ethics and practice entirely in terms of the coach's responsibility, which is to:

- discover, clarify and align with what the client wants to achieve;
- encourage client self-discovery;
- elicit client-generated solutions and strategies;
- hold the client responsible and accountable.

While holding 'the client responsible and accountable' may be in alignment with the coaching philosophy, coaching dilemmas may arise if coaches were to take personal responsibility for coachees' unethical behaviour. These issues will be explored further later in this chapter.

To summarise this section, the main aim of ethical guidelines is to protect coachees and the public from dangerous coaching practice (Law, 2005). The main objectives are to:

- benefit clients;
- ensure safety;
- protect clients;
- manage boundaries;
- manage conflict.

Translating the above objectives to a code of practice requires coaches or coaching psychologists to:

- do no harm;
- act in the best interest of their clients and their organisations;

- observe confidentiality;
- respect differences in culture;
- apply effectively the best practice in everything they do;
- help clients to make informed choices and take responsibility to improve their performance and well-being;
- recognise their own role.

Managing the multiple boundaries, relationships and conflicts is particularly important in coaching. It requires coaches to have ethical attitudes, knowledge and skills in handling their coaching relationship.

Most of the professional societies warn that members may be disciplined or expelled from the society if they are found to have violated the codes of ethics. However, apart from providing a long list of 'should do' in the codes of practice, most of them offer very little practical support in terms of coaching ethically. What is missing is the 'how to' in actually putting ethical principles into practical action. The BPS has a professional disciplinary board. However, its role may be diminished in light of the new regulations that regulate the title of registered psychologist by the Health Professional Council from July 2009. The BPS has an Ethics Committee, which meets regularly to provide a forum for each representational member to learn about ethical practice. At the time of writing they are developing a reference group, which may offer members a service in terms of ethics matters.

Ethics and coaching

While one may think that unethical practice in coaching may affect a few individuals, its ripple effect upon the financial impact could be on a global scale. Unethical coaching seldom makes the news headlines, while the rise and fall of large financial companies do. For example, Enron was formed in 1985 by Kenneth L. Lay, and in 2001 became the seventh largest company on Fortune 500 in America with 31,000 employees and a stock market value of US$35 billion. It was regarded as the most innovative US company. However, signs of cracks were showing in the facade as accounting problems emerged and it announced bankruptcy. It was reported that the management practice was poor. Investigation lawyers found that the managers were 'coached' to adopt the 'seagull management' approach towards their customers (Weissman, 2008). They made a lot of noise to the customers and then moved on. While the trial of Lay and Skilling began in January 2006, the implications and lessons learnt from the demise of Enron are more than financial. While Lay and Skilling were heavily to blame for the inept executives and management practices that led Enron into bankruptcy, the greatest legacy of the case may be the social and ethical impact on future business leaders. For those individuals who work in executive and management coaching may have a direct or indirect influence on those practices that lever business outcomes. The relationship between coaches and coachees, coachees and customers is a unique characteristic of the coaching practice, which defines the practice and underlines the importance of ethics in coaching, a so-called 'double triad relationship' (Law, 2006).

For instance, on the subject of maintaining a good coaching relationship, what should you as a coach do if you discover that your coachee is engaging in unethical accounting or management practice (as in the Enron case)? As a coach, the following ethical questions may arise:

- Should you respect your client's/line manager's/subordinates's autonomy and do nothing?
- Should you tell the coachee that it is wrong, even though he or she may not listen or that this may result in the termination of your coaching contract?
- Should you inform their line manager or director, even if it might affect the coachee's career such as job security or promotion?
- Should you report this to the higher authorities if the director did not listen?

Challenges and dilemmas in coaching relationships

Traditionally, the lack of involvement in ethics by coaches and their clients' organisations has generated a great deal of apathy among business coaches and coachees about ethical coaching. When someone brings up the topic of ethics, it tends to bring up cynicism, paranoia or even laughter (McDonald and Zepp, 1990). The challenge for coaches in ethical coaching relationships is to create coaching cultures that encourage integrity. To make this happen, coaches need to be the moral compass for stakeholders (including coachees and clients' organisations). This means that coaches should take personal responsibility for coachees' unethical behaviour.

To improve the involvement in ethics, it is important to create ethical cultures within an organisation. This happens as a result of the conscious effort by all stakeholders (including coaches, coachees and leaders in the organisation). It calls for frequent, scheduled conversations between coaches and coachees about what the standards of their performance and their organisations *really are*. Coaches must be willing to share governance responsibility with the stakeholders including coachees, their line managers, the chief executive officer and the board of directors. As a coach, you are expected to observe the code of ethics of your own profession, and also to set the ethical standard yourself, coach by example, constantly keeping your actions above reproach. During coaching sessions, coaches should talk through hypothetical scenarios with their coachees about possible ethical dilemmas. This is to ensure that the coachees will know what to do when they come up against those ethical dilemmas when the coaches are not around. Ethical coaching questions include:

- How ethical is your behaviour?
- How ethical is your organisation as a whole?
- How vulnerable are you within this complex relationship?
- What are the core values that define your organisation?
- What are the core values that define you as a person?

Coaching dilemmas

In contrast to the general belief that ethical coaching is simply doing the right thing, in practice this is not always obvious. Consider the case that is illustrated in Text Box 10.1.

Text Box 10.1   Case study about the sharing of a coaching experience

Fred, 46, was a business and a life coach working mostly in a one-to-one situation for private clients. Jane, 35, having been promoted to human resources director of a local authority, found herself lacking the confidence to speak up and work with fellow directors in other departments of the organisation. Jane sought coaching support from Fred in order to increase her confidence in the workplace. Fred successfully completed a programme of life coaching sessions with Jane, which helped her regain her confidence as exemplified by her improved performance and impressive presentation in the boardroom. Over the course of the coaching programme, Fred had developed a very good coach/coachee relationship with Jane. Even after the completion of the agreed coaching programme, Jane was happy to keep in touch with Fred on a friendly basis. They continuously met in an informal environment over coffee without any fees charged by Fred for coaching. As part of promoting his business, Fred was invited to give a talk on coaching at a conference. He was thinking of inviting Jane to go along to share her experiences directly at the conference. Fred asked Jane and she agreed to do so, even without payment. However, when he informed the conference coordinator about his intention, she told Fred that she had to seek advice from the Conference Committee in order to consider the ethical implications and to obtain suggestions for the kind of precautions that they might need to take.

Reflective question

- If you were the ethical officer on the Conference Committee, what would you do?

In business, it is usually a good idea to invite an ex-client to give a testimonial about one's standard of practice. However, in terms of exposing the client in a conference, which is an uncontrolled public environment, this may have implications for the coaching professional's code of ethics and conduct of practice. For example, there are standards of informed consent, and of privacy and confidentiality. As a professional coach, we should obtain the informed consent of our client for disclosure of confidential information. In the above case study, one could recommend Fred to get a copy of the signed consent form to cover his liability if he chose to disclose the client's information for whatever reasons.

The coaches should also restrict the scope of disclosure and ensure that all participants at the conference understand and respect this professional code and maintain confidentiality. To achieve this, all the delegates would need to be informed in advance. They may also be required to sign a confidentiality statement.

There are other ethical questions surrounding the above case study in terms of the appropriateness of maintaining the professional boundary between the coach and the coachee. Is it appropriate to continue a friendly relationship with an ex-client?

One needs to consider that even a consent form may not provide the rationale in terms of why the client should devote her unpaid time to attending the conference to support her coach. From a psychological perspective, this may be due to the 'transference' between the client and the coach. Its effect may carry on well after the ending of the psychological contract between the client and the coach (Law, 2007). The phenomenon of psychological 'transference' is a projection of the client's emotion onto the coach, which may be due to the power relationship between the coach and coachee – for example, the client may wish to please the coach by accepting the invitation.

Another question – can one guarantee that no damage would occur to the client by the questions asked or comments made by a third party such as participants at the conference? Alternative solutions include use of video and actors. However, videoing would provide a different feel, function and purpose in comparison with the actual presence of the person. Acting incurs further training and briefing to the actors. Whichever way, maintaining confidentiality, seeking clients' informed consent and ensuring that clients are not harmed are still the three pillars in making our ethical decision.

The above case study may sound extreme. This is deliberate. The dilemma has been constructed by putting together a number of real cases and abstracting them into a single case. Also, for confidentiality reasons, the names of the people are fictitious. It does though illustrate the 'nuts and bolts' of dilemmas. More importantly, it demonstrates the complexity of a coaching relationship that may develop and how one can use the professional code of ethics to guide one's thinking and decision making. Even in an ordinary situation when a coach is asked by a director (the budget holder) to coach a team of senior managers (the job holders) with an objective to improve their performance, a number of questions would still arise from the coaching perspective (see Law, 2003):

- Who are the clients?
- Whose benefit has priority?
- Whose interests is the coaching psychologist serving?
- What is the coach's ethical duty?
- What is the responsibility of the coaching psychologist to manage different values and interests between all the stakeholders?
- How are the differences managed?
- Is there potential for abuse of power?
- What are the issues of confidentiality?
- What are the implications of vicarious liability?

Laura Nash (1981) poses 12 questions to help managers address ethical dilemmas, which may be adopted into resolving coaching dilemmas as follows:

1 Have you defined the problem accurately?
2 How would you define the problem if you stood on the other side of the fence?
3 How did this situation occur in the first place?

4 To whom and to what do you give your loyalty as a coach, coachee and as a client of the organisation?

5 What is your intention in making this decision?

6 How does this intention compare with the probable results?

7 Whom could your decision or action injure?

8 Can you discuss the problem with the affected parties before you make your decision?

9 Are you confident that your position will be as valid over a long period of time as it seems now?

10 Could you disclose without qualm your decision or action to your supervisor, your colleagues, the clients, your family, society as a whole?

11 What is the symbolic potential of your action if understood or misunderstood?

12 Under what conditions would you allow exceptions to your standards?

Very often, it is about asking oneself the right set of questions. However, in practice this is not always easy, as in coaching, individuals do have their own blind spots (including coaches themselves). This is a situation where a consultation with one's supervisor would be extremely valuable.

Coaching ethically

The previous sections have shown that although many professional coaching organisations do have their own code of ethics, there are many challenges in actually putting those codes into practice in terms of coaching and managing coaching relationships. For example, how can coaches ensure that they continue to coach ethically, especially under certain novel conditions such as Internet coaching via emails, web cameras etc.

The increasing popularity and use of Internet technology has brought many ethical issues in coaching. For instance, the confidential information and coaching advice being given through those multi-media may not be secure. There are also concerns about coaches appearing on television to perform or demonstrate their coaching practice in reality television shows. For the obvious attraction of public relations, many coaches have been keen to accept invitations to appear on television and radio shows (relating to the case study mentioned earlier). There are also issues around getting informed consent, which may be compromised under the uncontrolled media. The coaching professional bodies so far have provided very little support or guidance in terms of coaching in the multi-media and on legal issues that might arise. There is a growing need for the professional organisations to provide members with advice on the use of the Internet and/or new multi-media, and their legal implications. There are also increasing demands from members for ethical coaching/training and ongoing supervision as part of their professional practice.

From the author's experience of conducting many workshops in ethics for coaches and coaching psychologists at conferences, a major barrier for coaches to participate in learning is the lack of awareness among coaches about the relevance and importance of ethics in their practice. In other words, many coaches are in the business of coaching where they are too preoccupied in making coaching work as a business enterprise, such as marketing, learning new techniques etc. Many do not see ethics as an important integral part of their coaching business. To ensure that an ethical approach can be implemented in real-life practice, coaches need to realise that ethics is really part of their coaching business. Business ethics has come to be considered a management discipline. McNamara (2008) notes that 90 per cent of business schools now provide some form of training in business ethics. Many benefits of applying ethics in the business can be readily translated into coaching benefits.

First, paying attention to coaching ethics can substantially improve the quality of the coaching relationship. Coachees would feel that their coaches have a high ethical standard and professionalism. This would increase trust and respect (the first ethical principle).

Attention to coaching ethics is especially important in the current tough economic climate. During times of change, complex conflicts or credit crunches, it is more important to have a moral compass to guide individuals (be they leaders, coaches or coachees) about what is right or wrong. Ethical coaching can help to maintain a moral course in turbulent times. Continuing attention to ethics through coaching would raise the awareness of coachees as to how they want to respond to challenges consistently and ethically. Moreover, ethical coaching is also good public relations; it promotes a strong public image. Of course, one should not simply use coaching ethically primarily for reasons of public relations. However, in terms of a business case, the fact that a coach or a coaching organisation regularly gives attention to ethical practice would portray a strong positive image to the public. Aligning coaching practice with ethical values is critical to effective marketing and public relations of the coaching business. Coachees (and customers) would look for those coaches who value people more than profit and coach with the utmost integrity and honour.

Ethical coaching can be applied to groups, and management or executive coaching in organisations. Embedding ethics as part of values as well as objectives via coaching can help build strong teams and increase productivity in organisations. The inefficiency and ineffectiveness in large organisations are very often caused by a huge disparity between their organisational values and those held by their employees. Ethical coaching helps to align coachees'/employees' values with the organisational values as their top priority.

Ongoing attention and dialogue regarding ethical values during the coaching/coachee interaction help to build a culture of openness, integrity and a learning community – critical characteristics of strong teams in an organisation. Be it in coaching or in the workplace, coachees would feel happier if they feel strong alignment between their values and those of the organisation in which they work. They would also improve their motivation and performance as well as interpersonal relationships.

Ethical coaching can support coachees' personal growth and meaning. A consulting company tested a range of executives and managers and found that the more emotionally healthy executives were, the more likely they were to score high on ethics tests (Bennett, 1991). The implication of this finding to coaching is that attention to ethics in the coaching relationship should help coachees face reality – both good and bad – in the society, the organisation and themselves. Coachees need to be empowered with a high ethical standard so that they feel more confident to deal with whatever comes their way.

A coach can be sued for breach of the coaching contract if they fail to comply with the promises that they made. So the gap between the stated code of ethics and actual coaching practice has significant legal as well as ethical implications. Many coaching professional bodies require their members to have a professional indemnity insurance policy. Ethical principles are often applied to practical issues, which then become legislation (for example, equal opportunity policies, equality acts and company acts with corporate social responsibility). Attention to ethics ensures that coaching practice is ethical. It is far better to incur the cost of mechanisms to ensure ethical practices during coaching practice than to incur costs of litigation later with the risk of financial loss as well as the loss of reputation. Ethical coaching would help avoid the error of omission. Attention to ethics allows coaches to detect ethical dilemmas early on so that they can be addressed. In short, ethical coaching is a preventive practice. It helps coach and coachee embed their values that are associated with quality, equality and diversity. A good coaching relationship is based on human values. These include trust between coach and coachee, coaching performance, evidence-based evaluation, feedback, reliability and review.

The processes of ethical practice should be similar to those in business such as the Institute of Business Ethics. Translating these into coaching practice, they can be summarised into the following 12 steps:

1 Declaration – An explicit code of ethics should be endorsed by both coaches' professional organisations (examples mentioned in the previous section) and understood by the coach, coachee and the client's organisation (stakeholders).
2 Integration – Produce a strategy for integrating the code

into the coaching practice, which should be brought to life in the interaction between the coach and the coachee.

3 Communication – Circulate the code to all the stakeholders.

4 Commitment – There should be a personal response from all the stakeholders to indicate their commitment to the code of ethics in practice.

5 Affirmation – The professional bodies of coaching should have a procedure in place for members regularly to demonstrate their understanding of the code and its applications in their practice (e.g. via CPD).

6 Contracts – Coaches could consider making adherence to the code obligatory by including it in all coaching contracts.

7 Regular review – The professional bodies should have a procedure for reviewing and updating the code.

8 Enforcement – All the stakeholders should be aware of the consequences of breaching the code.

9 Training – Training about the code of ethics should be available for the stakeholders. The training should include issues raised in the code in the coaching practice (i.e. not just theories and principles).

10 Translation – International coaching companies or professional organisations should ensure that the code is translated for use in overseas subsidiaries.

11 Distribution – Coaches should provide copies of the code to coachees and all the stakeholders.

12 Annual report – Coaching companies or professional organisations should include the code in their annual report so that stakeholders or members and the wider public know the organisation's position on ethical matters.

Coaches who practice ethically show in their attitude, values and practice: the value of diversity (cultural sensitivity), equality (balance of power) and a sense of purpose. These characteristics of the ethical coach and ethical coaching mirror those characteristics of ethical organisations (Pastin, 1986).

Summary of key concepts

This chapter has provided a strong case for both coaches and coaching professional bodies to do more, to take a more positive attitude and a more proactive role in bringing ethics to coaches and the public. There is a need for greater support from the professional bodies in terms of ethical practice and keeping their code of ethics and practice up to date, including working with the media and using Internet technology. To summarise, it is worth reminding the reader of the following ethical considerations (Law, 2006):

- Aim to serve coachees well.
- Be informed about legal and employment requirements that override limits on confidentiality for the particular context.
- Make these limits clear to coachees.
- Consider supplementing a verbal description of limits with a written contract.
- When practising with extended confidentiality, share on a 'need to know' basis.
- Be trustworthy.
- Discuss with coachees if breaking confidentiality is necessary.
- Prepare to work through conflicting-stakeholder value perspectives.
- Understand that helping coachees to act is much better than the coach having to act.
- Discuss the case with a supervisor, coaching colleagues and manager.
- Where there is a specific duty or legal requirement for disclosure to a third party, warn the coachee during the sessions that if they tell you more, you will be under an obligation to act.
- Understand that every coaching interaction has ethical value dimensions.

In conclusion, ethical coaching can improve trust in relationships between coach and coachees, individuals and groups. At a macro level, it can embed ethical values in organisations and societies. It can also strengthen the coherence of the ethical culture within the coaching profession and its clients' organisations. If we take more effort in promoting ethical practice in coaching, we should see greater consistency in standards and qualities of coaching practice among the coaching organisations in the future.

Reflective questions

- Is there a noticeable absence in the topic of ethics in conversation amongst coaches in your experience?
- Why do many business leaders, coaches and managers believe that ethics simply involves 'learning what is right or wrong, and then doing the right thing' (McNamara, 2008)?
- On reflection, do you think that you have ever acted unethically in your coaching practice?

References

Bennett, A. (1991) Unethical behavior, stress appear linked. *Wall Street Journal*, 11 April: B1.

Collins Essential Thesaurus (2006) 2nd edition. New York: Harper Collins Publishers.

Law, H.C. (2003) Applying psychology in executive coaching programmes for organisations. *The Occupational Psychologist*, 49: 12–19.

Law, H.C. (2005) The role of ethical principles in coaching psychology. *The Coaching Psychologist*, 1: 19–20.

Law, H.C. (2006) Ethical principles in coaching psychology. *The Coaching Psychologist*, 2: 13–16.

Law, H.C. (2007) The ethics column. *The Coaching Psychologist*, 3: 33–34.

McDonald, G.M. and Zepp, R.A. (1990) What should be done? A practical approach to business ethics. *Management Decision*, 28: 9–13.

McNamara, C. (2008) Complete guide to ethics management: an ethics toolkit for managers, at www.managementhelp.org/ethics/ethxgde.htm

Nash, L. (1981) Ethics without the sermon. *Harvard Business Review*, 59: 79–90.

Pastin, M. (1986) *The Hard Problems of Management: Gaining the Ethics Edge*. Chichester: Jossey Bass.

Rowson, R. (2001) Ethical principles. In F.P. Barnes and L. Mudin (ed.) *Values and Ethics in the Practice of Psychotherapy and Counselling*. Milton Keynes: Open University Press.

Singer, P. (1993) *Practical Ethics* (2nd ed., p. 10). Cambridge: Cambridge University Press.

The Free Dictionary (2008) Accessible at www.thefreedictionary.com

Weissman, A. (2008) Lesson learnt from Enron: a lawyer's perspective on business ethics. Keynote address at the 'Real World Real People, Professional Ethics Conference', 1–3 July, Kingston University, Surrey, UK.

Wordnet (2008) Accessible at http://wordnet.princeton.edu

Recommended books

Pastin, M. (1986) *The Hard Problems of Management: Gaining the Ethics Edge*. Chichester: Jossey Bass.

Singer, P. (1993) *Practical Ethics* (2nd ed.). Cambridge: Cambridge University Press.

11

The interpersonal relationship in the training and supervision of coaches

Peter Hawkins and Gil Schwenk

Introduction

Coaching is fundamentally a relational activity, both in terms of the content that is brought and the medium through which change is enabled. The majority of issues brought by individuals to coaching are about relationships. These may be relationships with team members, staff who report to them, clients and customers, key stakeholders etc. This in large part is due to the fact that the great majority of executives have risen to senior positions in their organisations, because of their technical competence and managerial skill, but then find that the most critical parts of their new role are in influencing and leading others, which require high levels of interpersonal and relationship skills, for which they have not had specific training or development.

Coaching also takes place within a relationship and part of the core skill of a coach is to learn how to work with the coaching relationship in a way that will have the maximum impact on the coachee's relationships. This is true for all types of coaching but is even more central in transformational coaching, which is different in approach to skill, performance and development coaching. With transformational coaching, the major focus is on what needs to shift in the coaching relationship live in the room, in order to help create a shift in the coachee, which will in turn create a shift in the relationship they are bringing to explore (see Hawkins and Smith, 2009).

So relationships are the focus of much of what is brought to coaching; be it life coaching or management coaching as well as the medium in which coaching happens. Executive coaching additionally has the added challenge that it always has two clients to serve: the individual or team that they are directly engaging with, and the organisation that is employing them to do the work. Both clients have expectations and needs of the coaching, which sometimes may conflict. The coach needs to attend to both clients and the relationship between them.

Our aim is to challenge the reader to consider the relationships that are under the visible surface, thus improving the effectiveness of coach training, coaching practice and supervision. Since relationships are at the heart of the professional practice, it follows that both the training and supervision of coaches need to be centred on relational learning. Not only does the training content need to include an emphasis on the nature of relationships and include suitable relational theory, but there needs to be careful attention to the process of relational practice in the training and supervision.

Consequently, this chapter will explore the centrality of interpersonal relationships to coaching, coach training and supervision. We introduce and expand on the CLEAR model of coaching and the seven-eyed model of supervision, both of which emphasise the importance of interpersonal relationships in the training and supervision of effective coaches.

Our core beliefs about the centrality of relationships

In our work over the last 25 years we have held a radical relational view of personal and organisational change. This has drawn on a number of writers and schools, including social constructivists, cultural anthropologists, field theory, inter-subjective and dialogic approaches in psychotherapy and counselling, but above all has been influenced by the writings and teaching of Gregory Bateson. Some of our core beliefs from this heritage include the following:

• The self does not reside in the individual as a fixed entity but is co-created in the web of relationships between

individuals and in the narratives created by the individual and by others about them.
- Knowledge and learning often lies in relationships, not within individuals. These may be relationships with other human beings, or relationships with animals, machines etc.
- Organisational culture lies not in individuals, but 'In the habitual relational pathways that have been laid down in an organisational system' (Hawkins, 1997).
- To facilitate or bring about change in an individual, team, organisation or system involves a shift happening in the relationship between the change enabler and their client. The change enabler is part of the field and therefore part of the change.

The 'intersubjective' approach holds that objective study of the inner world of another person is impossible. Meaning and understanding emerges in a dialogical relationship between at least two parties. This being so, the study of the deeper aspects of coaching requires coaches and consultants who can reflect on their own culture as well as their personal mindsets, emotions and motivations. The inter-subjective and dialogic approach has been developed in recent years by Stolorow and Attwood (1984, 1992), Stolorow *et al.* (1994, 2002) and Donna Orange (1995).

Stolorow and Attwood (1992: 33) divides the unconscious into three realms:

(1) *the prereflective unconscious* – the organizing principles that unconsciously shape and thematize a person's experiences;
(2) *the dynamic unconscious* – experiences that were denied articulation because they were perceived to threaten needed ties;
(3) *the invalidated unconscious* – experiences that could not be articulated because they never evoked the requisite validating experience from the surround.

All three types of unconscious can form parts of what Bollas (1987) describes as the 'unthought known' – that which we experience but have not yet been able to make sense of or articulate. This division can be helpful in coaching in assisting coaches to:

- understand the organising principles that frame how they are experiencing the world;
- facilitate the individual in speaking their truth when appropriate and overcoming fears that are historically rooted;
- provide validation of the subjective experience of the coachee through active, empathic listening.

The relational aspects of coach training

It is essential that coach training mirrors the interpersonal relationship of the coach–coachee relationship in order to ensure that it is relevant and effective. Trainees learn as much if not more from the implicit curriculum and the medium of the training as they do from the explicit content. This can be accomplished in several ways.

Coach training should include a significant proportion of practice coaching within a safe learning environment. This should be 'real play' rather than 'role play'. 'Real play' is coaching on real situations or issues that the coachee is currently facing. Our own training courses allocate the majority of time to work in threes where each trainee takes on the role of coach, coachee and observer. The coachee works on their real current issues, and the coach has to find ways of relating that will create a shift in the here-and-now relationship that will impact on the relationships that are being brought for exploration.

Our core coaching process model called the CLEAR model has five stages, each requiring different relational skills. In this model the coach starts by **Contracting** with the coachee on both the boundaries and focus of the work. Then the coach **Listens** to the issues that the coachee wishes to bring, listening not only to the content, but also to the feelings and the ways of framing the story that the coachee is using. Before moving on, it is important that the coach lets the coachee know that they have not only heard the story, but have also 'got' what it feels like to be in their situation. Only then is it useful to move on to the next stage to **Explore** the dynamics of the relationship with the coachee as well as what is happening in the coaching relationship live in the room, before facilitating the coachee to explore new **Action**. Finally, there is a **Review** of the process and what has been agreed about next steps.

We will now reflect on some of the relational skills necessary for each of these stages. **Contracting** is the foundation of effective coaching. We believe that effective executive coaching requires three-way contracting between the coach, the coachee and the organisational client. Many coaches who do this refer to the coachee 'sponsor'. We talk instead about 'the representative of the organisation' as they are responsible for making sure that the organisation learns and benefits from this coaching relationship. They are not just there to support the coachee in their learning but also to have an important role in linking the coaching back to the wider systemic learning.

The relational aspects of contracting are illustrated in the following dialogue:

COACH: What would success look like from this coaching?

COACHEE: I would be less assertive and controlling in my interactions with my team and peers.

COACH: How would this benefit you and the others?

COACHEE: I wouldn't kill potentially good ideas before they have been developed and tested.

COACH: What are the consequences on the relationships with your team and peers when you kill the ideas before they have been developed and tested?

COACHEE: It separates me from the others and I am perceived as someone who others don't want to work with.

COACH: So, by improving the controlling behaviour, you want to develop better working relationships that enable other ideas to develop and flourish.

Effective **Listening** builds trust and helps the coachee develop greater levels of understanding and awareness. As indicated by Table 11.1, a primary objective of coach training is to help the coachee to listen at a deeper level, so that the coachee is enabled to learn and understand more profoundly than they could have without the assistance of the coach.

However, we believe that understanding and awareness is insufficient for a real change in the coachee unless there is a 'shift in the room'. This is often experienced as a physical shift in how the coachee is sitting or a noticeable change in non-verbal expression. This can be grounded through dialogue about the implementation of action. Often, we encourage coaches to use 'fast forward rehearsal' to visualise and embody the future actions that the coachee will take.

The **Explore** stage of the coaching relationship is nurtured through a process of skilful questions and listening. Powerful questions are core to this part of the coaching process as they enable the coachee to explore the situation from

Table 11.1 Objectives of coach training

Level of listening	Activity of listener	Outcome in the person being listened to
Attending	Eye contact and posture demonstrate interest in the other.	'This person wants to listen to me.'
Accurate listening	Above plus accurately paraphrasing what the other is saying.	'This person hears and understands what I am talking about.'
Empathic listening	Both the above plus matching their non-verbal cues, sensory frame and metaphors; feeling into their position.	'This person feels what it is like to be in my position. They get my reality.'
Generative empathic listening	All the above plus being able to play back and shape the emerging story that the coachee is sharing.	'This person helps me to hear myself more fully than I can by myself.'

different perspectives, facilitating new insights, options and possibilities. Good coaching questions include:

- **closed questions** – seeking data ('How many apples do you have?');
- **open questions** – seeking information ('Why did you plant apple trees?');
- **leading questions** – seeking information and indirectly suggesting how they want the question to be answered ('Why do you like apples best?');
- **inquiry questions** – inviting active inquiry ('What are the criteria for judging the best apple?');
- **transformational or mutative questions** – inviting active inquiry that not only assists the coachee in thinking outside their current frames and mindsets but also creates an emotional shift in the person being asked ('What would it take for you to begin to like apples?').

The **Action** stage requires the relational skills of inviting the coachee, not just into talking about what they might do differently, but also embodying that change live in the coaching relationship.

COACH: So you are committed to confronting this issue with your colleague when you meet with them next Tuesday. Can you show me how you are going to do that by talking to me as if I am the colleague?

COACHEE: Ummm ... I realise that I often dominate our meetings and do not give the space for others' ideas to take shape before I criticise them. I really need your help in challenging me when I do this.

This would be followed by direct feedback from the coach and an opportunity to do a second or third rehearsal. What the coach is focusing on here is not the coachee getting their 'lines right', but creating an authentic embodied shift in how they are relating to this person. This will manifest in breathing, posture, eye contact, language, metaphor and other ways in which they are engaging differently (Hawkins and Smith, 2009).

One of the key skills for the final CLEAR stage of **Review** is the ability to give and receive feedback that is clear, owned, regular, balanced and specific. Typically, feedback sessions on coach training take 50 to 100 per cent as much as the coaching session itself. Since we do most of our coach training in threes, we normally start with the coach providing feedback on him or herself, followed by the coachee and finally by the third person of the triad giving their perspective as observer. In all cases, we focus on what the coach did well and also what they could do to improve in the future.

A relational approach to coaching supervision

Role and purpose of supervision

Supervision is a key element both in the training process for coaches and also in lifetime continuing professional development. In training it is the process of rigorous supervision that helps the trainee link the theory and skills they learn on courses to the real-time experience of working live with coachees. In workshops you can learn models and develop competencies, and begin to practice being an effective coach through working with your peers, but these do not by themselves produce an excellent coach. Supervision provides the reflective container for the trainee to turn their competencies into capabilities and to develop their personal and coaching capacities.

We propose elsewhere that supervision has three basic functions: *qualitative, developmental* and *resourcing* (Hawkins and Smith, 2006). The qualitative aspect is assisting the individual coach to provide the best possible professional coaching to their coaches. The developmental function is attending to the continuing personal and professional development of the coach, which helps them to increase their capacity as an action learner and reflective practitioner by going right round the learning cycle and reflecting on their current relationships with coaches. This will help them to gain new insight; shift their current models, theories and coaching methods; plan and practise new ways of engaging their coaches and take that back into new practice. The resourcing function is the need to attend to the whole person of the coach and how they are resourcing and supporting themselves to continue to be effective in the role.

These three functions are all critical to delivering some of the key outcomes of the supervisory relationship. We see these as being:

- providing the continuous professional development and action learning of the coach or mentor (developmental);
- helping the coach or mentor to develop their internal supervisor and become a better reflective practitioner (developmental);
- providing a supportive space for the coach or mentor to process what they have absorbed from their clients and their client's system (resourcing);
- helping keep the coach and mentor honest and courageous and attending to what they are not seeing, not hearing, not allowing themselves to feel or not saying (qualitative);
- looking at where and how the coach or mentor may need to refer the client on for more specialised help (qualitative).

The stages in a supervision session

We use a similar process model for supervision to the five-stage coaching model CLEAR (**Contract, Listen, Explore, Action, Review**), although these skills, within the context of supervising another coach, are different and build on the basic coaching skills. In supervision, the supervisor not only has to serve the needs of the coachee and their organisation, but also has a duty of care to the coaches of their supervisee and has an obligation to the wider profession. This needs to be reflected in the contracting.

The seven-eyed coaching model: a process model of supervision

In the late 1980s, Peter Hawkins and Robin Shohet (Hawkins and Shohet, 1989) developed a more in-depth model of supervision, which later became known as the seven-eyed supervision model, and has been used across many different people professions in many countries of the world. Peter Hawkins adapted this supervision model for Shadow Consultancy in 1998 and in 2006 Hawkins and Smith (2006) adapted it for coaching and mentoring.

Its purpose is to explore the various different influences on supervisory activity in the room. It is based on both a systems and a relational understanding of the ways things connect, inter-relate and drive activity. This model also integrates insights and aspects of intersubjective psychotherapy, focusing on the inter-relationship between the internal and relational life of individuals. We will now set out in more detail these seven areas of potential focus for supervisor and supervisee in reviewing their practice (see Figure 11.1).

The model reinforces the interpersonal aspect of coaching and supervision since it is based on two complementary systems. The first relationship is the coach–client system and the second relationship is the coach–supervisor system. These are explained in detail below.

Mode 1 The coachee's system

Here the focus is on the content of the session in the coachee's system, the problem the client system wants help with and how they are presenting the issues.

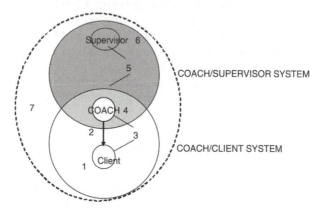

Figure 11.1 Seven modes of supervision

The supervisor's skill in this mode is to help the coach accurately return to what actually happened in the session with the coachee – what they saw, what they heard and what they felt – and to try and separate this actual data from their preconceptions, assumptions and interpretations. It is also useful for the coach to be helped to attend to what happened at the boundaries of their time with the coachee, their arrival and exit, for it is often at the boundaries that the richest unconscious material is most active.

Typical mode 1 questions might include:

- Think back to the last session with this client. What had happened just before the session?
- What did the client look like as they came into the session?
- How did the session start?
- How did the client present him/herself during the session?
- What did you see, hear and feel during the session?

Mode 2   The coach's interventions

This looks at how the coach relates to the coachee, how they work through each stage of the CLEAR process in the session and what interventions the coach made, including alternative choices that might have been used. It might also focus on a situation in which the coach is about to intervene, exploring the possible options and the likely impact of each.

Sometimes coaches will ask for help with an impasse they have arrived at in facilitating the change process. They will often present this impasse in the form of an 'either/or' question such as: 'Should I collude with this situation or confront the issue?' The skill of the supervisor is to avoid the trap of debating the either/or options, and instead to enable the coach to realise how they are limiting their choice to two polarised possibilities and facilitate a shared brainstorming that frees up the energy and creates new options. Then the benefits and difficulties of these options can be explored and some possible interventions tried out in role-play.

Mode 2 questions might include:

- What options were you thinking about for handling this situation?
- What else might you have tried?
- What is the wildest intervention you could use?
- Who else do you know who would handle this well? What would they do?

Mode 3 The relationship between the coach and the coachee

Here the focus is neither solely on the coachee and their system nor the coach, but the relationship that they are creating together. It is here that the relational aspect of supervision first comes to the core by moving the focus from (a) the coachee and their world and (b) the activity of the coach, as well as attending to the relational field, both conscious and unconscious.

The supervisor has to facilitate the coach in standing outside the relationship that they are part of and see it afresh, from a new angle. The Chinese have a proverb that the last one to know about the sea is the fish, because they are constantly immersed within it. In this mode the supervisor is helping the coach to be a flying fish, so they can see the water in which they are normally swimming.

In mode 3, we want the coach to become aware of the relationship with the coachee. This can be done through asking them to describe the relationship and discover new sub-unconscious elements through the use of metaphor and simile. We might ask:

- How would you describe your relationship with this client?
- What other relationship does this remind you of?
- If you and this client were marooned on a deserted island, what would happen?
- If you and this client were to go to a fancy dress party as a couple or pair, what would symbolise the relationship?

These mode 3 questions can also be used to get a better understanding of the coachee's relationships. The supervisor could use similar questions to understand the relationships with key individuals in the coachee's relational web. So, if the focus of the coaching is about the relationship of the coachee and his/her manager, the supervisor could ask:

- From what you have heard and understand of the client, what does his/her relationship with his/her manager remind you of?
- From what you have heard and understand of the client, if the coachee and his/her manager were marooned on a deserted island, what would happen?

Mode 4   The coach

Here the focus is on the coach beginning to look at themselves, both what is being re-stimulated in them by the coachee's material, and also themselves as an instrument for registering what is happening beneath the surface of the coaching system.

In this mode the supervisor helps the coach to work through any re-stimulation of their own feelings that has been triggered by the work with this client. Having done this the coach can be helped to explore how their own feelings may be very useful data for understanding what the coachee and their system is experiencing but is unable to articulate directly. The coach also explores how their own blocks may be preventing them from facilitating the coachee and their system to change.

Questions in this mode would be:

- What feelings does this coachee re-stimulate in you?
- Who do they remind you of?
- When have you been in a similar relationship dynamic?

Mode 5   The supervisory relationship

Here the focus is on what is happening in the relational field between the coach and the supervisor. This includes both the conscious aspects of how they are relating and the 'parallel process' (Hawkins and Shohet, 2006; Hawkins and Smith, 2006). A parallel process occurs when the coach unconsciously absorbs a range of feelings and ways of relating from the coachee system. It then may be being played out in the relationship with the supervisor. The coach can therefore unawarely treat the supervisor in the same way that their coachee treated them or indeed demonstrate how they engaged the coach, by engaging the supervisor in the same way.

Here the supervisor needs to be able to attend not only to what they are being told about the coaching system, but also to what is happening in the relationship in the room. Having acquired this skill, the supervisor can then at times offer their tentative reflections on the impact of the presented material on the coaching relationship to illuminate the coaching dynamic. When done skilfully, this process can help the coach bridge the gap between their conscious understanding of the coaching relationship and the emotional impact it has had on them.

In mode 5 a supervisor might say:

- When you discuss this client we become very argumentative and both our voices speed up and get louder – and I wonder whether this reflects something about the coaching relationship?
- I notice every time we discuss this client I become very sleepy and bored and wonder what that is about?

Mode 6 The supervisor self-reflection

The focus for mode 6 is the supervisor's 'here and now' experience while with the coach and what can be learnt about the coach/coachee relationship from the supervisor's response to the coach and the material they present.

In this mode the supervisor has to attend not only to presented material and its impact on the 'here and now' relationship, but also to their own internal process. The supervisor can discover the presence of unconscious material related to the coaching relationship by attending to their own feelings, thoughts and fantasies while listening to the presentation of the coaching situation. These can tentatively be commented on and made available as possible indicators to what lies buried in the relationship with the coachee. The additional skill is to have a means of sharing this with the coach in a non-judgemental and speculative way. For example, the supervisor might say:

- I am aware that my heart is beating faster as I hear you telling this and I am feeling quite agitated by the situation.
- I feel sad and empty as I listen to this.

Mode 7 The wider context

The focus of mode 7 is on the organisational, social, cultural, ethical and contractual context in which the coaching and supervision is taking place. This includes being aware of the wider group of stakeholders in the process that is being focused on. These may be the client organisation and its stakeholders, the coach's organisation and its stakeholders, and the organisation or professional network of the supervisor.

The supervisor has to be able to bring a whole system's perspective to understand how the systemic context of the work being presented is affecting, not only the behaviour, mindsets, emotional ground and motivations of the coach and coachee, but also themselves. The skill is to appropriately attend to the needs of the critical stakeholders in the wider systems, and also to understand how the culture of the systemic context might be creating illusions, delusions and collusions in the coach and in oneself. Attention to mode 7 also requires a high level of transcultural competence (see Hawkins and Shohet, 2006; Hawkins and Smith, 2006).

Some mode 7 inquiries might include:

- What have you learned from the client about the values and assumptions operating in the organisation? How is this demonstrated in the relationship between coachee and the manager/peer/customer etc.
- How is conflict handled in the organisation? In this particular coachee relationship?
- Who are the main stakeholders that you heard about in the sessions? How would you describe the coachee's relationship with each?
- How are these stakeholders connected?

- How are wider political, economic and social pressures being enacted in the relationships you are working with?

Using all seven modes

In talking to both supervisors and coaches who have gone to others in search of help in exploring coaching situations, we have discovered that often different supervisors are stuck in the groove of predominantly using one of the seven modes of working. Some focus entirely on the situation 'out there' with the coachee and adopt a pose of pseudo objectivity (mode 1). Others see their job as coming up with better interventions than the coach managed to produce (mode 2). This can often leave the coach feeling inadequate or determined to show that these suggested interventions are as useless as the ones they had previously tried. Other coaches have reported taking a problem with a coachee and having left supervision feeling that the problem was entirely their pathology (mode 4).

'Single-eyed vision', which focuses only on one aspect of the process, will always lead to partial and limited perspectives. This model suggests a way of engaging in an exploration that looks at the same situation from many different perspectives and can thus create a critical subjectivity, where subjective awareness from one perspective is tested against other subjective data.

Each mode of supervision can be carried out in a skilful and elegant manner or ineffectively, but no matter how skilful one is, a single mode will prove inadequate without the skill to move from one to another. We have devised a training method for helping the supervisor use each of the modes with skill and precision and to explore the timing and appropriateness for moving from one mode to another.

The most common order for moving through the modes is to start with mode 1 by talking about specific coaching situations. Then to move into modes 3 and 4 to explore what is happening both in the coaching relationship and for the coach/supervisee. This may well lead to an exploration of the here-and-now relationship in the room between the coach and the supervisor (modes 5 and 6), and/or bring into awareness the wider context (mode 7). Finally, having gained new insight and created a shift in the supervisory matrix, the attention may turn back to mode 2, to explore what different interventions the coach might use in their next session to create the needed shift in the coaching matrix. The coach might even try out some of these interventions in what we term a 'fast-forward rehearsal'. From our experience we have learnt that if the change starts to happen live in the supervision, it is far more likely to happen back in the coaching.

The model has also been used as a way of empowering the coach, who is the customer receiving the supervision, to be able to give feedback on the help they are being given and request a change of focus. It can thus be used as a framework for a joint review of the supervision process by the coach and supervisor.

Conclusion

Interpersonal relationships, the space between individuals, are the essence of organisations and systems. The effectiveness of one's relationships is a major determinant of success in business, family and social systems.

The interpersonal relationship between a client and coach provides a space of challenge and support in the service of transforming the relational effectiveness in the systems in which the coachee operates. Likewise, supervision provides a space for the coach to explore their coaching relationships so that they have a better awareness and understanding of the client and the client relational systems.

Thus, interpersonal relationships are frequently central to the purpose of the coaching. Interpersonal relationships are the medium of effective coaching training and supervision. Transformed interpersonal relationships are an important outcome of coaching, training and supervisory relationships.

The 'hidden curriculum' of all coach and supervision training and supervision is to be adept at providing attention to the relational field. This means that supervisors and trainers need to be comfortable reflecting live on the relationships in the training and supervisory room, and be open to their own process and practice being part of that which is explored and commented upon.

Reflective questions

- Do you agree that both the training and the supervision of coaches need to be centred on relational learning?
- Is it essential that coach training mirrors the interpersonal relationship of the coach–coachee relationship?
- Have you asked for help from your supervisor with an impasse you have encountered in facilitating the change process? How was it dealt with?

References

Bollas, C. (1987) *The Shadow of the Object: Psychoanalysis of the Unthought Known*. London: Free Association Books.

Hawkins, P. (1997) Organizational culture: sailing between evangelism and complexity. *Human Relations*, 50: 417–440.

Hawkins, P. (2009) Coaching supervision. In E. Cox, T. Bachkirova and D. Clutterbuck (eds) *The SAGE Handbook of Coaching*. London: Sage.

Hawkins, P. and Shohet, R. (1989; 2nd ed. 2000; 3rd ed. 2006) *Supervision in the Helping Profession*. Maidenhead: Open University Press/McGraw-Hill.

Hawkins, P. and Smith N. (2006) *Coaching, Mentoring and Organisational Consultancy: Supervision and Development*. Maidenhead: Open University Press/McGraw-Hill.

Hawkins, P. and Smith, N. (2009) Transformational coaching. In E. Cox, T. Bachkirova and D. Clutterbuck (eds) *The SAGE Handbook of Coaching*. London: Sage.

Orange, D. (1995) *Emotional Understanding*. New York: Guilford Press.

Stolorow, R.D. and Attwood, G.E. (1984) *Structures of Subjectivity: Explorations in Psychoanalytic Nominology*. Hillsdale, NJ: Analytical Press.

Stolorow, R.D. and Attwood, G.E. (1992) *The Context of Being: The Intersubjective Foundations of Psychological Life*. Hillsdale, NJ: Analytical Press.

Stolorow, R.D., Atwood, G.E. and Brandchaft, B. (1994) *The Intersubjective Perspective*. Northvale, NJ: Jason Aronson.
Stolorow, R.D., Atwood, G.E. and Orange, D. (2002) *Worlds of Experience*. New York: Basic Books.

Recommended books

Hawkins, P. and Shohet, R. (1989; 2nd ed. 2000; 3rd ed. 2006) *Supervision in the Helping Profession*. Maidenhead: Open University Press/McGraw-Hill.
Hawkins, P. and Smith, N. (2006) *Coaching, Mentoring and Organisational Consultancy: Supervision and Development*. Maidenhead: Open University Press/McGraw-Hill.

Final reflections

Stephen Palmer and Almuth McDowall

While putting together edited books such as this one comes not without challenges for the editors, the clear benefit is that there is just so much to be learned from the writing and knowledge of the individual contributors. Reading and editing the respective chapters it became evident that a number of different themes link these contributions, even if they appear individualistic and quite different from each other at first glance:

1 *Issues to do with the relationship itself*: the second chapter puts much-needed emphasis on what coaching has in common with other relationships, and how it differs. This shows clearly that relationships are more effective with high commitment from all parties involved, and where the role of the 'helper's self' is clear and constructive.

2 *The way we communicate in relationships*: Chapters 6, 8 and 9 highlight the role of language and discourse in the coaching relationship. The same words may be interpreted differently across those involved in coaching, and coaches may in fact play an active role in facilitating alternative meanings. Chapter 9 also highlights how important it is to set clear boundaries, and communicate and review at regular intervals.

3 *Factors or processes that may change or affect relationships in some way*: Chapters 4 and 5 highlight that the use of additional sources of information is often integral to the coaching process. Coaches may use different types of assessment tools, and feed the outcomes or indeed other

information back to the coachee. These processes clearly have their place in coaching relationships, but need to be handled with sensitivity and care.

4 *The wider context of coaching relationships*: no relationship exists in a vacuum. Chapters 7, 10 and 11 highlight that there is a wider context for effective coaching relationships. Coaches should be appropriately trained, and supervision is put forward as an appropriate mechanism for continuous professional development. The issue of culture and diversity is acknowledged, as most coaches will at some point in time be working with coaches whose background might be quite different from their own. Ethics are still a relatively new and, dare we say, under-represented area in coaching, but absolutely vital to protect the interests of all involved.

The chapters also offer additional food for thought. To illustrate this point, Chapter 3 frames the coaching relationship in terms of the 'psychological contract' and the 'coaching alliance'. This highlights that relationships are formed in our heads, even before initial contact might be made, as people come to any relationship with a whole set of expectations and assumptions. Chapter 7 on culture questions some of these assumptions, such as our inclination to adopt a rather categorising approach to national culture, and calls for more inclusiveness.

While the chapters are all rooted in research, not all evidence is from research on coaching. While looking to other areas of psychology and social sciences is fruitful and can provide rich cross-fertilisation, we nevertheless end with a 'call to arms' to all coaches and coaching psychologists to help build an evidence-based framework for refining our understanding of interpersonal relationships in coaching. We know that we *should* be putting people first, but quite *how* we do this could be developed further. As a critical example, there is no research on ethical boundaries in coaching, which is in stark contrast to the volume of evidence in business ethics. While we appreciate that this type of research is sensitive and difficult to conduct, it is nevertheless sorely needed in order to protect all parties' interests in an informed manner.

We are aware that this book has not provided easy answers to relationships in coaching. However, we hope that it has helped to raise our readers' understanding of their complexity and to raise their self-awareness. This, we purport, is the key to 'putting people first'. To conclude, we leave our readers with final reflective questions:

- What is your 'psychological contract' with regards to coaching relationships? What are your expectations? Where do these come from?
- How can you ensure that you 'put people first' in the coaching relationship in terms of the processes, techniques as well as language and dialogue that you use?
- Which wider issues are important to you as a coach, such as training, supervision and adherence to ethical standards? What is this saying about you as a coach?

Glossary

360-degree assessment: Process where an employee is rated on criteria agreed in advance by a number of different sources such as coworkers, their manager, subordinates and occasionally customers.

360-degree feedback: Process where one individual (employee or coachee) receives *feedback* from various sources, such as managers, co-workers and customers.

Ability test: Test that measures a person's mental capacity.

Appreciative Enquiry: Paradigm from the social sciences, which holds that people invest meaning through language. If language is positive and directed towards what could be, this facilitates change.

Appropriate Responsiveness (in relation to coaching): An iterative process involving doing what is necessary in the interpersonal coaching relationship to produce positive or beneficial change dependent on the perspective of the conceptual approach and the purposes of the coachee and coach.

Aptitude test: Test that measures a specific or several specific abilities.

Assessment: Process of evaluating something or someone else, in the context of coaching usually the coachee, using criteria defined in advance, such as actual job data from performance appraisals or particular scales in *psychometric tools*.

CLEAR: This is an acronym that stands for Contract, Listen, Explore, Action and Review. First developed by Peter Hawkins in the 1980s, the model can be applied to both coaching and coaching supervisory contexts.

Coaching: The art of facilitating the unleashing of people's potential to reach meaningful, important objectives.

Coaching alliance: This reflects the quality of the coachee and coach's engagement in collaborative, purposive work within the coaching relationship, and is jointly negotiated and renegotiated throughout the coaching process over time.

Common Factors approach: A major thrust of the psychotherapy integration movement, the Common Factors approach asserts that certain common factors are key to successful psychotherapy outcome across conceptual approaches. The most consensual commonality is the development of a therapeutic alliance.

Common Factors comparison: In addition to psychotherapy, other change-inducing dyadic social relationships have been compared in the literature on the basis of common factors, in seeking those commonly helpful (or harmful) processes of change.

Communication system: The network of meaning and action that connects contextual experiences (action) with contextual narratives (meaning).

Complex Adaptive Systems: Types of systems that are in themselves whole systems, and that adapt to and interact with other whole systems, e.g. the coaching relationship.

Contextual experience: Fragments and patterns of action that show themselves in episodes of communication.

Contextual narratives: The stories, assumptions, beliefs and expectations that we form individually and collectively out of our experience.

Contracting, the process of: Contracting is an active process that is revisited throughout the coaching alliance. Initial assessment is followed by regular reviews that reinforce commitment and realign the coaching work. Ending is the final stage of the process, but is described and discussed from the outset.

Criterion-orientated approach: An assessment is used to measure individual characteristics with regard to a particular outcome (e.g. does this assessment tell me that the coachee can do the job well?).

Cultural orientation: The inclination to think, feel or act in a way that is culturally determined.

Culture: A group's culture is the set of unique characteristics that distinguishes its members from another group.

Derailment: Refers to when an employee, usually senior, starts performing below expectations or even behaves in counterproductive ways.

Evidence-based coaching psychology approach: 'the intelligent and conscientious use of best current knowledge in making decisions about how to deliver coaching to coaching clients, and in designing and teaching coach training programs' (Cavanagh and Grant, 2006: 156).

Feedback: Communication process, where a feedback message is transmitted from the recipient to the sender. Feedback can originate from the self, others or the task.

Feedback message: Information that is conveyed from one party to another during a feedback process.

Feedback recipient: The individual that receives any feedback; in the context of this book, usually an employee or the coachee.

Feedback sender: The individual or individuals who are giving feedback to someone else.

Feed forward: Process where through questioning a positive frame of mind is facilitated first, then actions are directed towards the future, before finally conveying any feedback information.

Game Theory: With applications in the domains of management, sport, social and behavioural sciences, Game Theory is an inter-disciplinary approach to the study of human behaviour, often in the areas of conflict and cooperation. Using the analogy of a game, interactive and iterative situations between two or more 'players' can be modelled.

Global coaching: A holistic approach, calling on multiple perspectives (one of which being culture) both for choosing meaningful, important objectives and for effectively reaching them.

Goal Setting Theory: Cognitive psychological theory that in essence holds that goals direct and sustain action; harder goals are more likely to motivate (but should be achievable).

Individual difference: Personal characteristic that is related to sets of behaviour, such as someone's level of self-esteem or self-belief.

Influence: The capacity within an individual to affect the behaviour and/or beliefs of others.

Inter-national coaching: Coaching across national boundaries.

Intra-national coaching: Coaching diverse individuals in one country (e.g. in a cosmopolitan metropole, in an international organisation).

Key Performance Indicators: These refer to targets or goals set for an employee as part of the annual appraisal or review process.

Leveraging cultural differences: Making the most of cultural differences; achieving a synthesis, unity in diversity.

Means: The Means is the activity the coachee engages in with the intention of bringing about certain Ends or goals. **Ends**, which are the actual outcomes of the adopted Means, may be quite different from the idealised Ends for which the Means were adopted at the outset.

Motivational Interviewing: 'a person-centred, non-directive method of communication, which works collaboratively with the coachee supporting them to enhance their intrinsic motivation towards personal behavioural change, by helping them resolve their historical amibivalence to the change that they face' (Passmore and Whybrow, 2007).

Neuroticism: One of the scales of typical personality measures that taps into 'emotional stability', i.e. how we deal with stresses from the environment but also our own emotions.

Performance appraisal: Also often called 'review', this refers to a process of assessing an employee in an organisation against specified criteria, goals or objectives (or a mixture of these).

Personality: Set of enduring, stable characteristics of an individual.

Possible self: Beliefs of what the 'I' is like and could be like, these could be positive or negative.

Power: The propensity within human beings to impose their will on others.

Precipitating factors: Problems and challenges that arise during the coaching engagement from developments in the lives of the coachee or the coach, the relationship between them or indeed the client organisation. These could not have been anticipated at the start of the relationship.

Predisposing factors: Issues in existence (for coach or coachee) before the coaching alliance began and which could have an impact on the success of the relationship.

Profiling approach: The measurement of particular attributes (e.g. strengths and weaknesses) of an individual.

Psychometric tools or instruments: Assessment instruments that are objective and scored in a particular standardised way. These should be reliable and measure a valid construct.

Reflexive agency: The ability to notice the assumptions and effects of one's behaviour and to make conscious, situated choices and decisions in the communication system that reflect and develop the complexity of business contexts that are being acted out of and into.

Relationship stage models: Relationships are dynamic and appear to move through a number of clearly defined stages as they change and mature.

Self-efficacy: The belief that one has in one's capabilities ('to what extent am I capable of doing this?').

Seven-eyed model of coaching supervision: The seven-eyed model was developed by Peter Hawkins and developed first with Robin Shohet and the Centre for Supervision and Team Development and then with Nick Smith in the field of coaching. It is formed of two interacting systems – the client–coach system and the coach–supervisor system. The seven eyes or modes are different perspectives that the supervisor can use to direct the focus of a supervisory conversation.

Systems (in the context of Complexity Theory): A group of interdependent elements making up a whole that is greater than the sum of its parts and that unfolds over time (see Cavanagh, 2006).

Timeline or lifeline: Tool used in coaching and counselling where the individual is asked to draw a line showing 'highs' and 'lows' in their life, and annotate this with comments.

References

Cavanagh, M. (2006) Coaching from a systemic perspective: a complex adaptive conversation. In D.R. Stober and A.M. Grant (eds) *Evidence Based Coaching Handbook: Putting Best Practices to Work for Your Clients*. Hoboken, NJ: John Wiley and Sons.

Cavanagh, M.J. and Grant, A.M. (2006) Coaching psychology and the scientist practitioner model. In D.A. Lane and S. Corrie (eds) *The Modern Scientist-Practitioner: A Guide to Practice in Psychology*. London: Routledge.

Passmore, J. and Whybrow, A. (2007) Motivational interviewing: a specific approach for coaching psychologists. In S. Palmer and A. Whybrow (eds) *Handbook of Coaching Psychology: A Guide for Practitioners*. London: Routledge.

Web resources

Association for Coaching
Association for Coaching is an established professional body. Link to their Codes of Ethics and Good Practice: www.association forcoaching.com/about/about02.htm

Association for Professional Executive Coaching and Supervision
Association for Professional Executive Coaching and Supervision is a professional body specialising in executive coaching. Link to ethical guidelines: www.apecs.org/coachingEthicalGuidelines.asp

Bath Consultancy Groups
An organisation development consultancy: www.bathconsultancy group.com

Brief Therapy Practice
Brief Therapy research list: www.brieftherapy.org.uk/research.php

British Psychological Society Psychological Testing Centre
British Psychological Society Psychological Testing Centre provides reviews of psychometric tests: www.psychtesting.org.uk

British Psychological Society Special Group in Coaching Psychology
The British Psychological Society (BPS) Special Group in Coaching Psychology is a member network of the BPS: www.sgcp.org.uk

Buros Library of Mental Measurements
The Oscar K. Buros Library is a specialised reference library containing publications of the Buros Institute, and what is generally regarded as the world's largest collection of tests and testing materials: www.unl.edu/buros/bimm/html/library.html

Centre for Supervision and Team Development
Consultancy and training provider: www.cstd.co.uk

Chartered Institute of Personnel & Development
The Chartered Institute of Personnel & Development has a factsheet on 360-degree feedback, as well as more general guidelines on performance appraisal feedback: www.cipd.co.uk

Coaching & Mentoring Relationship Research
This website maintains list of coach–coachee and mentor–mentee publications which are relevant to this chapter: www.coaching relationshipresearch.webs.com

Coaching Across Cultures
See the Crossing Across Cultures website for the book (2003) and seminars developed by Philippe Rosinski: www.coachingacross cultures.com

Cultural Orientations Framework (COF)
A questionnaire has been developed based on the Cultural Orientations Framework (COF) by Philippe Rosinski, described in his book *Coaching Across Cultures* (2003): www.philrosinski.com/cof

European Mentoring and Coaching Council
The European Mentoring & Coaching Council (EMCC) exists to promote good practice in mentoring and coaching across Europe: www.emccouncil.org

Geert Hofstede's research
Geert Hofstede's research on cultural differences: www.geert-hofstede.com

The Higher Education Psychology Academy Network
You can download many good presentations and articles regarding feedback. These are from an educational context, but have content highly relevant to coaching, including a bulletin on using feedforward and feedback by Sally Brown: www.psychology.heacademy. ac.uk

International Association of Coaching
The International Association of Coaching is an independent, global, coach-certifying body. Link to codes of ethics: www. certifiedcoach.org/ethics.html

International Coach Federation
The International Coach Federation is a professional coaching

body. Link to Codes of Ethics: www.coachfederation.org/includes/
redirects/articlecount.cfm?articleID=280&filename=code.doc

International Test Commission
www.intest.org

Simply 360
Free online handbook for human resources managers: www.
simply360.co.uk/handbook/

Society for Coaching Psychology
The Society for Coaching Psychology is a professional body for
coaching psychologists. Link to Code of Ethics: www.
societyforcoachingpsychology.net/page_1208006102984.html

Society for Intercultural Education, Training and Research (SIETAR)
SIETAR is the world's largest interdisciplinary network for professionals working in the intercultural field: www.sietar-europa.org

Index